A Touch of Heaven

Finding New Meaning in **Sabbath Rest**

GREGORY P. NELSON

Pacific Press® Publishing Association
Nampa, Idaho
Oshawa, Ontario, Canada

Edited by Kenneth R. Wade
Designed by Tim Larson
Cover photo by John Baker

Copyright © 1999 by
Pacific Press® Publishing Association
Printed in the United States of America
All Rights Reserved

ISBN 0-8163-1721-6

99 00 01 02 03 • 5 4 3 2 1

Contents

For my parents, Paul and Barbara,
who showed and taught me that the Sabbath is a day of delight.

And for my wife, Cindy,
and my three teenage children, Vaughn, Natalie, and Julian,
who have journeyed with me in playing heaven with the Sabbath.

Chapter 1

Needed: Spiritual Renewal in the Church

You've heard of the experiment involving the frog and the kettle? Place a frog in boiling water, and it'll jump out immediately because it can tell that it's in a "hostile" environment. But place a frog in a kettle of room-temperature water, and it'll stay there, content with those surroundings.

Slowly, very slowly, increase the temperature of the water. This time, the frog does not leap out but just stays there, unaware that the environment is changing. Continue to turn up the burner until the water is boiling. The poor frog will be boiled, too—quite content, perhaps, but nevertheless dead.

Is it possible that the Christian community, the church, is in danger of ending up like this frog? Is the church succumbing to the secularism of its surrounding environment, becoming comfortable with the status quo? Instead of being in the world but not of the world, has it become more *of* the world rather than just *in* the world? Is it becoming intimidated and captured by the culture and, consequently, having minimal impact?

On the surface, the shape of the church in North America seems quite good. As Charles Colson observes, "We live in a time that would seem to be marked by unprecedented spiritual resurgence: 96 percent of all Americans say they believe in God; 80 percent profess to be Christians . . . 50 million Americans claim to be born again." Not a bad showing for the church!

But Colson goes on to point out that there are 100 times more burglaries in so-called "Christian" America than in so-called "pagan" Japan. So he asks, "Why this paradox between profession and practice? Why is the faith of so many not making an impact on the moral values of our land?"[1]

Surprisingly, Anglican Bishop Michael Marshall suggests that the problem with contemporary Christianity in America is that many people have settled for a "facsimile" of Christianity: They are trying to run their own lives while at the same time saying they believe in Christ. He calls this brand of religion "decaffeinated Christianity— it promises not to keep you awake at night."[2]

How can this happen? What produces decaffeinated Christianity? Perhaps George Gallup provided a partial answer when in a survey conducted several years ago he revealed that while 95 percent of the population believe in God and 80 percent embrace the divinity of Jesus, only a minority of 40 percent express their beliefs through consistent church attendance; and although 72 percent claim to accept the Bible as the Word of God, only 15 percent claim to read it on a daily basis; 24 percent admit that they never open it at all.[3]

Christians get more exposure to the secular culture than to the spiritual culture. When as many as a quarter of professing believers never even open God's Word, and almost a half do not regularly experience corporate worship and praise, this suggests that values and beliefs are being shaped by the secular environment. Is the church in danger of being captured by the culture?

Tragically, our youth aren't exempt from the "frog in the kettle" syndrome either. Dean Borgman, professor and youth ministry expert, recently wrote: "The gap between the mores of Christian and church kids and those of the general culture is much narrower than ever before. Your kids are more into materialism and relativism of the world and more of them are indulging in sex and drug highs than you think."[4]

In the 1980s the Seventh-day Adventist Church conducted a large study called Valuegenesis, focusing on the faith, values, and commitment of Adventist youth grades 6 to 12.[5] More than twelve thousand youth, one thousand nine hundred parents, and over seven hundred pastors, teachers, and principals participated, making this study the largest ever of its kind in any denomination. Valuegenesis takes an in-depth look at the three major institutions responsible for educating youth: families, congregations, and schools—identifying the dynamics within each that promote faith maturity, Christian values, and loyalty to the church among youth.

The study revealed some very encouraging trends among Adventist youth, showing the positive contributions that families, churches, and schools are making. But in the midst of the successes, the report pointed out some significant concerns that must be addressed.

For example, to the question "How important is religious faith in your life?" only 15 percent of the youth (grades 6 to 12) said it was the most important influence in their life, 34 percent said it was a very important influence in their life, and another 35 said it was an important influence, but other things also were important in their life.

In the area of congregational climate, 36 percent of our youth said they look forward to going to services at their church, and only 50 percent said they go to their church because they want to attend.

To the question "When you are forty years old, do you think you will be active in the Adventist church?" just 27 percent of the youth (grades 6 to 12) said there was an excellent chance, 45 percent said there was a good chance, and 19 percent said a fair chance.

It's obvious the church has a challenging road ahead in addressing the significant issues relating to faith maturity, Christian values, and loyalty to the church among the youth. And when Adventists' responses were compared to other denominations', Adventist youth weren't far off, which is to say that none of us can pat ourselves on the back at this point and feel that the job is over.

The Christian church in North America is in significant need of spiritual renewal. Not only do we face the tremendous task of reaching and keeping our own members, we are confronted with the enormous challenge of invading our secular culture with the gospel of Jesus Christ—a culture whose prevailing consensus is that God is unnecessary.

Donald Posterski paints the picture this way:

The idea that God is not central in this world is seeded in your mind before your feet hit the floor in the morning. The preset alarm on the bedside radio brings you the news from the night before. There's an update on a war going on somewhere. Closer to home there has been an overnight rape and murder, firefighters are containing a blaze at a paint factory, and there is no end in sight for the strike that is in its fourteenth day. The news concludes with a little political rhetoric, a human interest snapshot, a short weather report, a long sports report, and a warning about a serious accident that has caused a major traffic tie-up. God is never mentioned. He doesn't matter.

"God has not been declared dead in the modern world; He has just been displaced. God is the forgotten one, on the sidelines of everyday life. Certainly, many would admit, He still exists. It's just that He is unnecessary. Optional . . . God has been demoted."[6]

In spite of the fact that much of the media and Hollywood's recent material involves religious themes, their picture of God remains far from compelling and even distorting.

Take the recent popular movie *City of Angels*. Set in the bustling metropolis of Los Angeles, the story graphically portrays how an angel named Seth comes to fall in love with a beautiful surgeon named Maggie.

But in order for the angel to actually be able to experience this love, to feel the warmth of touch, the sensations of taste and pleasure that human beings enjoy, he must choose to give up his existence as an angel by throwing himself off a high place (and so becoming a "fallen" angel). It's an untenable choice, really: eternity or earth, the world of angels or the world of human beings.

He chooses the latter, for the sake of a woman's love. It's a "touching" choice, a moving portrayal (especially since it involves Nicholas Cage and Meg Ryan in the roles). So they finally fall in love and experience their love together. At last, real joy!

But like most Hollywood stories, the tragic happens. This beautiful surgeon, now the love of his life, dies in an accident. He's left alone on this earth after choosing to join the earth. His life is crushed.

Sitting in his living room one night, Seth's former "colleague," an angel partner, appears to him. "If you'd known this was going to happen, would you have done it?" the angel asks.

With tears streaming down his face, Seth replies, "I would rather have had one breath of her hair, one kiss of her mouth, one touch of her hand, than an eternity without it. One!"

Beautiful sentiments. Unfortunately, incredibly distorting! The whole concept in this movie is that to really enjoy life and experience it to the full, you must separate yourself from God. If you want the abundant life, you don't need God.

That's the tragic value system of our culture. God is around, but He's removed from real life, in essence, unnecessary. In subtle whispers and with bold accolades, our culture chants, "You don't need God to make it in life!" Unfortunately, as we've seen so far, the church is in danger of being captured by this culture. Unless we take some bold, decisive steps to reverse this trend, we will be adrift in the seas of secularism, with people being unable to distinguish between the values of the world and the church.

George Barna sounds the clarion call when he observes that we are in a pivotal decade in the history of American Christianity. It's a time in which the church will either explode with new growth or quietly fade into a colorless thread in the fabric of a secular culture. The changing nature of our society has pushed us past the point of simply being able to mark time.

"In this decade, Christianity must prove itself to be real and viable, or become just another spiritual philosophy appearing in the history of mankind."[7]

The church is in desperate need of renewal. And the good news is that it has been given a gracious gift by God to help facilitate this revitalization, a gift eternally designed to turn us back to the Father and into His arms of love.

Frederick Buechner tells the poignant story about a boy of twelve or thirteen who, in a fit of crazy anger and depression, took a gun and fired it at his father.[8] The father died soon afterward. When the authorities asked the boy why he had done it, he said that it was because he couldn't stand his father. Dad demanded too much of him, he was always after him for something. "I hate my father!" the young boy said defiantly.

Later on, after the boy had been placed in a house of detention, a guard was walking down the corridor late at night when he heard a sound from the boy's room. The guard stopped to listen. The boy was sobbing out in the dark, "I want my father, I want my father!"

That, says Buechner, is a kind of parable of the lives of us all. Modern society is like that boy in the house of detention. We've killed off our Father. Our narcissistic, self-centered view of life has made God unnecessary. We're more concerned with ourselves and what happens to us than about Him.

As a result, we hurt deeply inside without Him. Perhaps without us realizing it, our souls are crying out, "I want my Father, I want my Father!" Deep down inside, isn't that the cry from the soul of society?

Bertrand Russell, the renowned atheist, once said, "The center of me is always and eternally a terrible pain—a curious wild pain—

a searching for something beyond what the world contains."[9] We've been created with a need for God, and without Him, there is a painful aching and longing for something more. If the church stops its busy activities of kingdom-building long enough to look carefully and listen closely within and without, it will hear those lonely cries coming from lonely people.

The world only offers the untenable choice, eternity or earth, a colorless life without warmth and pleasure or earth with warmth and pleasure. It's one or the other. What a tragic solution to human angst: Choose God *or* enjoy real life.

God longs for His children to enjoy the intimate fellowship with Him that He's already restored through His Son Jesus Christ. He has given us a remarkable gift to help bring that about. It's a gift that when taken seriously and experienced fully can facilitate genuine renewal and revitalization both individually and corporately. The gift is His Sabbath rest. Explore with me now what it is about this gracious gift that can bring revival and renewal. Entering into His Sabbath rest will help the tattered and battered hearts of this world find true rest and peace, even in the midst of the battles and crises of life. The Father's Sabbath rest will bring emotional, social, physical, and spiritual renewal. Let's see how.

Chapter 2

The Touchstone
of Spirituality

A Jewish preacher had a reputation for delivering very pointed sermons about the judgment. One Sabbath, he preached particularly strongly about the horrible consequences of breaking the Sabbath and how God would treat such sinners. Then, as his custom was, the next day he went from home to home of his parishioners collecting contributions for his preaching.

He soon came to the house of one of his members who had the reputation of being the worst Sabbath breaker in the synagogue. This man notoriously kept his business open every Sabbath. And yet, to the preacher's surprise, the man welcomed him warmly and contributed generously.

"Praise God," the preacher proclaimed. "God has brought you to repentance to see your sinful ways and stop you from desecrating His holy day!"

The storekeeper replied, "Oh no, rabbi! I'm being generous to you today, not because of repentance, but because of gratefulness to you. You see, your fiery sermons against Sabbath breaking will undoubtedly inspire other businessmen to close their shops on Sabbath, and that will leave me with less competition!"[1]

The storekeeper's attitude toward the Sabbath reveals his attitude toward life in general: Life is lived in competition with others; so whatever it takes to get ahead is the thing to do. Ironically, the Sabbath for him was a means to that end.

It is true that one's attitude toward the Sabbath seems to be a touchstone of overall spirituality. A touchstone is "any test or criterion by which to measure a thing's qualities."[2] The Sabbath as a touchstone is a measure of the quality of spirituality.

Notice how a number of authors have picked up on this quality of the Sabbath. Theodore L. Gardiner writes, "The Sabbath law comes nearer to being *a true measure of our spirituality* than any other, and it was oftener made a test of loyalty by God Himself than was any other precept."[3]

M. L. Andreason several times emphasizes this symptomatic quality of the Sabbath: "He who takes the Sabbath away, takes worship away . . . and greatly impoverishes spiritual life. . . . Sabbath keeping is an accurate barometer of spiritual life."[4] In another place, he writes again that Sabbath breaking is a symptom of spiritual decline, of departure from God, of estrangement from the promise, of a sickly Christian experience. "Let this be emphasized: it is a symptom indicative of disease, and reveals an inward condition of apostasy from God. . . . Sabbath keeping is . . . *a gauge of our friendship and fellowship with God."* [5]

Richard M. Davidson, chairperson of the Old Testament department at the Seventh-day Adventist Theological Seminary, at Andrews University, states that far from being the one commandment that is ceremonial and not moral, as some claim, the Sabbath is a test of the highest morality—to worship God totally, without reservation, because we trust what He says. "The Sabbath is the litmus test of what man will do with all moral law. It is the measure of our whole posture toward all of God's expectations. Here is the ultimate test in interpersonal relations."[6]

How can these authors make such sweeping statements about the Sabbath? How can one's attitude toward the Sabbath be a barometer of one's spirituality?

Prior to his previous statement, Davidson shows that the commandment to keep the Sabbath cannot be scientifically, or with simple, mental reasoning, proven to make sense. Why? The seven-day week, ending with the Sabbath, has no relationship to any cyclical changes of nature or movements of heavenly bodies; whereas the daily, monthly, seasonal, and yearly cycles can be scientifically calculated with precision. Consequently, the seventh-day Sabbath as the climax of the week exists simply because God declared it so! So the Sabbath is "the moral nerve center of the law."[7] In other words, how we relate to the Sabbath is symptomatic of how we relate to God and what He says.

Oswald Chambers wrote:

> There is only one thing God wants of us, and that is our unconditional surrender. . . . [Have] simple perfect trust in God, such trust that we no longer want God's blessings, but only want Himself. Have we come to the place where God can withdraw His blessings and it does not affect our trust in Him?[8]

So the question is, Are we able to do something simply because God asks us to? Sabbath and our attitude toward it is a gauge of that willingness.

Both Andreason and Gardiner give the same reason for why the Sabbath can be the touchstone of spirituality. God gives the Sabbath as a day for fellowship with Him; therefore our relationship to that time is indicative of our desire for meaningful fellowship with Him—it becomes a kind of test of our loyalty to Him and how much we value Him.

As Andreason says, since the Sabbath provides opportunity for worship, meditation, reflection, study, prayer, communion, and fellowship, when we neglect these experiences or seriously interfere with them, our religion ceases to be effective, and worldliness takes the ascendancy. "For this reason Satan considers the overthrow of the Sabbath one of his best means of causing men to forget God, and of lowering the spiritual tone of the people. As men forget the Sabbath, they forget God."[9]

This certainly was the case with the children of Israel during Old Testament times. From the very beginning, God had told them that the Sabbath was to be the sign that He was their God and that He had chosen them to be His people and that they had all willingly entered into a beautiful covenant relationship together (Exodus 31:16, 17; Ezekiel 20:12, 20). So every time they entered into the Sabbath celebration, it was, "in a sense, a renewal of the covenant relationship."[10] Keeping the Sabbath was not simply an external affair; it was a spiritual attitude as well, serving as an indicator that the eternal covenant relationship was still in existence. By their faithful observance of the Sabbath celebration, the people were in effect saying to God, "We belong exclusively to You, and we're glad about it! We're proud to be your children, and we would have it no other way!"

Years later, after apostasy after apostasy, the prophet Ezekiel, speaking to Israel on God's behalf, points out to them (20:13, 16, 21, 24) that "the profanation of the Sabbath . . . [is] a major sign of [their] refusal to acknowledge [their] God as Lord, Saviour, and protector. It is an external manifestation, in addition to others, that she has broken the covenant."[11] It is a sad indication that they no longer want to be exclusively God's.

What happens when people forget God? Ezekiel goes on to connect their breaking of the Sabbath with their apostasy into idolatry. Notice that progression: "They rejected my laws and did not follow my decrees and desecrated my Sabbaths. For their hearts were devoted to their idols" (v. 16).[12] And again the same sequence: "They had not obeyed my laws but had rejected my decrees and desecrated my Sabbaths, and their eyes [lusted] after their fathers' idols" (v. 24). Notice, with the use of the word *lusted*, the allusion to the concept of spiritual adultery. Sabbath breaking is in effect saying to God, "We no longer want to be exclusively Yours. We want to be able to have affairs with other lovers." This concept of the Sabbath will be addressed in greater detail in chapter 9.

So it appears to be true that when people forget the Sabbath, they forget God. In the words of the great Augsburg Confession, Article XXVII: "In neglecting the memorial of creation, the Sabbath, men are liable to forget both the God of creation and creation itself."[13]

Ellen White affirms this reality when she writes: "Had the Sabbath been universally kept, man's thoughts and affections would have been led to the Creator as the object of reverence and worship, and there would never have been an idolater, an atheist, or an infidel."[14]

The Sabbath is indeed a touchstone of spirituality. "It is set as the perpetual guardian of man against that spiritual infirmity which has everywhere led him to a denial of the God who made him, or to the degradation of that God into a creature made with his own hands."[15]

One of the outstanding religious leaders of American Judaism, Mordecai Kaplan, in summing up the unfortunate situation of the decline of spirituality in modern Judaism, makes an interesting observation:

> What, then, has weakened the Jewish sentiment that was so strong a feature in the maintenance of the synagogue in the past? Many elements, undoubtedly, have contributed to the undermining of that sentiment, but chief of all is the dwindling of Sabbath observance. Kept away from attendance at the synagogue on the traditional day of rest and common worship, the Jew finds little motive for being identified with the synagogue, and, when he finds himself out of touch with synagogue life, it cannot be long before he becomes entirely

cold to Jewish traditions and ideals. Hence, among the principal measures for the upbuilding of the synagogue must be the restoration of the Sabbath.[16]

It would appear then that Rabbi Kaplan also sees the renewal of spirituality and the renewal of the church coming about with a renewal of the Sabbath experience. Could it be because it is on the Sabbath that corporate worship takes place that facilitates the believer's identification with the church and its community of believers? Indeed, the Sabbath is a touchstone of spirituality.

If this is all true, then the questions that should be addressed are, What is it about the Sabbath that facilitates this spiritual renewal in the life of the believer? How could the understanding and keeping of a day bring about spiritual renewal in the church? It all revolves around what that *day* stands for.

Chapter 3

Rekindling
the Blaze

In Alexander Solzhenitsyn's now famous sermon to America, delivered in 1978 at Harvard University, he told the American people that we have placed too much hope in politics and social reforms, only to find out that we were being deprived of our most precious possession: our spiritual life. It is trampled by the party mob in the East, by the commercial one in the West. We are, he thundered, at a "harsh spiritual crisis and political impasse. All the celebrated technological achievements of progress, including the conquest of outer space, do not redeem the twentieth century's moral poverty." We need a "spiritual blaze."[1]

A "spiritual blaze." Why? It doesn't take long, when one looks around and observes people, when one looks deep inside, to see that the fire of passion for life often dies down to a few sputtering embers threatened to be extinguished by the winds and rains of our hurricane existences. Life is so fast-paced, hurried, and harried. Our worlds are consumed with conflicting priorities and incessant demands for decisions that have to be made now "or the offer is off!" As one author said, "Busyness . . . is endemic to our culture. . . . Most of us have taximeters for brains, ticking away, translating time and space into money."[2]

We need a "spiritual blaze." Why? Henry David Thoreau described it: "The mass of men live lives of quiet desperation." People still walk around, says Brennan Manning graphically, they still perform all the gestures and movements that we identify as human. But the fire inside of them has died. "They have lost the vision. They have lost what Boris Pasternak calls 'the inward music.' They are zonked spectators carried along on a mechanical sidewalk, like travelers at the Atlanta airport."[3]

We need a "spiritual blaze." Why? So often our endless rounds of busy activities are anything but meaningful. "What's the point of it all?" we say in hopeless frustration. "Surely there must be something more to life than what I'm experiencing."

Could it be that the media and Hollywood have picked up on this existential cry and for this reason are offering so many programs and movies that deal with spirituality and religious themes? But the question is, are their solutions adequate?

Manning puts his finger on the drudgery of our lives when he writes that there are three ways of committing suicide—taking my own life, letting myself die, and letting myself live without hope. "This last form of self-destruction is so subtle that it often goes unrecognized, and therefore unchallenged. Ordinarily it takes the form of boredom, monotony, drudgery, feeling overcome by the ordinariness of life."[4]

No wonder people, in their quest to transcend the ordinary, look for more and more excitement that will catapult them beyond boredom and hopeless monotony. A new generation of roller coasters, for example, are being ridden by thousands of people searching for that ultimate thrill—The Desperado in Las Vegas plunges from 209 feet in the air into an underground tunnel, at more than ninety miles per hour. Other roller coasters put human bodies through nearly the same gravity load as the space shuttle astronaut's experience.

"The aim is to build in every bit of fright imaginable. Riders want it," explains coaster designer Ronald Toomer. He's right. Greg Blum, fifteen years old, from Dallas, Texas, bounded off the Texas Giant roller coaster at Six Flags Over Texas, and breathlessly said, "That was almost too much to stomach! Let me on again."[5]

Obviously, roller coasters are only one evidence that people are attempting to bring greater excitement to their lives. It's just symbolic of our modern desperate hope that there must be more to life than what we are experiencing.

But, as Gordon MacDonald wrote, "Leisure and amusement may be enjoyable, but they are to the private world of the individual like cotton candy to the digestive system. They provide a momentary lift, but they will not last."[6]

We need a "spiritual blaze." Why? Unless the subsurface of the soul within every person is given careful attention, there is no adequate support for the stresses in the real world. MacDonald illustrates it this way.

The asphalt road on which he drives the last few miles to Peace Lodge, his family's New Hampshire retreat, is beautiful in the fall. In the early spring, though, the road looks like a disaster area. FROST HEAVES, a sign explains to drivers in late March as the ground begins to thaw on warm days.

Each day the road seems to buckle more and more until it has the properties of an old washboard. Here and there potholes open up where water has seeped in and frozen in the night air. The car tires beat the road surface into chunks, and before long the entire length of Shaker Road is a mess. It occurred to him one day that while Shaker Road was like that in the early spring, the connecting State

Route 106 was not. In fact, it was as smooth as glass, a pleasure to drive, spring or fall. What made the difference between the two?

The road repair gang gave him the simple explanation one day. When Route 106 was constructed, the work crew had carefully laid a thick bed of gravel beneath the roadbed that provided the necessary drainage. The bed was deep enough that it was untouched by the cold going into the ground or the frost coming out of it.

Shaker Road, on the other hand, was completely different, the men told him. There, the ground had simply been graded and a thick patch of asphalt laid over it. "A quick and dirty job," someone said. With an inadequate bed, the road was torn up every spring by the moisture underneath that worked into every crack and made the sub-surface unreliable. The car and truck tires did the rest.

"If I do not give attention to the subsurface [of my life]," MacDonald concludes, "the cracks and strains will quickly show the minute the surface changes or stresses occur."[7] How important it is for us to give careful attention to the subsurface, our inner spirit, making sure it is strong enough and properly maintained so that it can support the stress of the real world.

We need a "spiritual blaze." The only answer to an exhausted, passionless, stressed-out, hope-drained life is to check the condition of the subsurface, the inner spirit. That's where Sabbath, the still time, comes in. As Marva Dawn puts it, "In an age that has lost its soul, Sabbath keeping offers the possibility of gaining it back. In an age desperately searching for meaning, Sabbath keeping offers a new hope."[8] A new hope of what?

The Sabbath offers the good news that living without hope, suicide, does not have to be the only answer. From the very beginning human beings were created with the capacity and need to hope for something better, to dream of life's possibilities and to reach out and touch them. How did it happen?

At the climax of Creation week, God shared His own rest with the man and woman He had personally shaped and formed. By that gracious gift of the Sabbath, He was declaring His friendship with the human race, His determination to connect our destiny with His own. Now that gives reason for hope.

From that time on, every Sabbath would announce the universe's greatest promise, every Sabbath would build and create hope in hearts of believers, that we have more, not less, to expect from the future because God has graciously given us the gift of intimacy and friendship with Him. That's what the Sabbath says. Connected to Him, all things are possible! Hope is everything.

Victor Frankl, a famous Vienna psychiatrist, saw in a German concentration camp the significance of hope. One day a fellow prisoner confided to him that a voice in a strange dream had promised to answer whatever question he wanted to ask. The man said he'd asked to know when the camp would be liberated, and the dream voice said March 30. The man awakened from his dream absolutely thrilled and excited—March 30 was just a few weeks away.

Under the torturous conditions in the camp, the man took the dream seriously, believing with all his heart that March 30 would bring salvation. But as the day approached and the news reaching the prisoners remained discouraging, the man took sick. On March 31—after the deadline, after his hope had shattered—the man died. The physical cause was typhus, but Dr. Frankl believes it was the sudden loss of hope, the severe disappointment, that lowered the man's resistance to the infection. The experience, along with many others, convinced him that if you have nothing more to expect from life, you begin to lose it.[9]

That's why the Sabbath is so important for us! It brings us weekly reassurance and hope that our origin and destiny are rooted in God. It provides us with "a sense of continuity with the past and a hope for the future. It invites us to rest in God while living in a restless middle and waiting for that end (yet endless) rest and peace of God (Heb. 4:9) for which we were created."[10]

We need a "spiritual blaze." It's the Sabbath and all it stands for that can rekindle those dying embers into a blaze of spiritual passion and vitality.

Let's take a closer look now at what it is about the Sabbath and the experience of Sabbath keeping that fuels the flames of spirituality. How can the Sabbath facilitate spiritual renewal?

Chapter 4

Vacationing With God

William Wilberforce, a committed Christian, was a member of the English Parliament in the early years of the nineteenth century. One of the great contributions he made as a politician was his vigorous leadership in helping to convince Parliament to pass a historic bill outlawing slavery in the British Empire.

This was no small feat. It took him almost twenty years to put together the coalition that eventually passed the antislavery measure. Pages and pages of detailed documentation of the injustices and cruelties of slavery were painstakingly compiled during those years. Lawmakers who were afraid to offend the interests of big business had to be skillfully persuaded. Wilberforce had his enemies, too—political foes who would have loved to see him fall.

Wilberforce's spiritual strength and moral courage had to be immense. An incident that took place in 1801, some years before the antislavery measure was passed, gives insight as to the source of his strength and courage. Lord Addington had led his party into power, and as the new prime minister, he had begun to form a new cabinet.

The central issue of the day in England was peace; Napoleon was terrorizing Europe, and the concern was whether or not England could stay out of war. Wilberforce was rumored to be among the top candidates for a cabinet post, and because of the peace policy of Lord Addington, Wilberforce was most anxious to gain the appointment. Garth Lean, one of Wilberforce's biographers, tells the story:

It did not take long for Wilberforce to become preoccupied with the possibility of the appointment. For days it grabbed at his conscious mind, forcing aside everything else. By his own admission he had "risings of ambition," and it was crippling his soul.[1]

But now comes the secret to Wilberforce's spiritual stamina. There was a disciplined check and balance to his life, a routine that was indispensable. As Lean says, "Sabbath brought the cure." Wilberforce's check and balance to a busy life was Sabbath; he had come to understand genuine rest and its importance. He had discovered that "the person who establishes a block of time for Sabbath rest on a regular basis is most likely to keep all of life in proper perspective and remain free of burnout and breakdown."[2] Sabbath rest.

Commenting about two other politicians who both committed suicide during that time, Wilberforce wrote in his journal, "With peaceful Sundays, the strings would never have snapped as they did from overtension."

No wonder the great spiritual father, Thomas Aquinas, centuries ago, perceptively referred to the Sabbath rest as "a day of vacation with God."[3] Vacationing with God. What a concept! Who would not want to spend time with a God like that!

What is it about vacations that are so appealing? A break from the routine; a chance to do what you haven't had time to do; spending time with people you love; rest and relaxation; renewal. We all need vacations—times to live without being captive to time.

A certain trumpet player always lived without a watch or clock. Whenever he would be given one, he would hock it or sell it. He said, "I don't need a timepiece. I live in an apartment house, and when I want to know what time it is, especially during the night, all I have to do is start blowing scales on my trumpet, and it ain't long before someone yells out their window, 'Hey, what's the idea, playing that thing at 3:30 in the morning?!' "[4] Living without time—not worrying about watches. Calvin Miller, in his book *The Table of Inwardness,* says that intimacy with God can't be rushed, that we can't enjoy the presence of God if we're always looking at our watches. That's why the Sabbath is so important.

Vacationing with God, Sabbath rest, brings spiritual renewal. But why? Where did the idea of this Sabbath rest come from?

Twice it says in Genesis 2:1-3 that "[God] rested." Notice when and where this took place: "Thus the heavens and the earth were completed in all their vast array. By the seventh day God had finished the work he had been doing; so on the seventh day he rested from all his work. And God blessed the seventh day and made it holy, because on it he rested from all the work of creating that he had done."

"[God] rested." The picture is repeated in Exodus 31:15,17: "For six days, work is to be done, but the seventh day is a Sabbath of rest, holy to the Lord. . . . It will be a sign between me and the Israelites forever, for in six days the LORD made the heavens and the earth, and on the seventh day he abstained from work and rested" (NIV).

"[God] rested." What an unusual picture. God tired from His work of creation? God exhausted and needing rest? God stopping to catch His breath?

Looking at the way many Christians approach the Sabbath, one would think that was God's need—Lay Activities time. Unfortunately, by focusing primarily on the element of physical rest on the Sabbath, the tremendous value of God's idea of rest has been missed.

Does God indeed need to rest? Of course not! But did God choose to rest? Yes. Why? Because, as MacDonald observes, "God subjected creation to a rhythm of rest and work that He revealed by observing the rhythm Himself, as a precedent for everyone else. In this way, He showed us the key to order in our private worlds."[5]

Notice the divine rhythm of rest and work, night and day, grace and law. From this basis it is possible now to explore how this Sabbath rest facilitates spiritual renewal. Let's define this Sabbath rest a bit more. There's a twofold Sabbath rest: resting from our works in order to rest in God's works.

Chapter 5

Resting From
Our Works

Samuele Bacchiocchi provides an intriguing insight on this first element of Sabbath rest. He says that in the Near Eastern creation myths, the divine rest, which usually implies the establishment of a secure world order, is generally achieved either by eliminating noisy, disturbing gods or by creating humankind.

For example, in the Babylonian creation epic *Enuma Elish*, the god Marduk says, "Verily, savage-man I will create. He shall be charged with the service of the gods, that they might be at ease!"

So in the Babylonian stories, God rests because human beings make it possible. But notice that in the biblical story, it's the other way around: Human beings rest because God makes it possible.

"In the creation Sabbath, the divine rest is secured not by subordinating or destroying competitors, nor by exploiting the labor of mankind, but rather by the completion of a perfect creation."[1] In other words, God rested on the seventh day, not to conclude His work of creation but rather because His work was "finished . . . done" (Gen. 2:2, 3).

God's rhythm of work and rest revolves around the acknowledgment of His perfect creation, His completed work. "He regarded it as complete and perfect, and to acknowledge it—God stopped."[2] In other words, God does the work, human beings enjoy the results.

What's the implication of this for our spiritual renewal? First, entering into God's Sabbath rest means resting from our works in order to enjoy God's completed work. Adam's and Eve's very first full day was the Sabbath rest with God, by His gracious invitation—before they had any opportunity for work (Gen. 1:27-2:3).

Adam and Eve had nothing to offer to God on their first day with Him except their willingness to spend time with Him, accepting His gift of rest for them, His gift of fellowship with them, accepting as a gift the beautiful creation He had finished and perfected for them. They couldn't present anything they had done. All they could do was to view what God had done for them. Consequently, "they approached the Sabbath empty-handed of any human merit." "They were invited to rest not because of anything they had done, but because God had finished His work."[3]

The Sabbath, then, was a day in which they entered into God's already completed, perfect works for them. What a time of celebration it must have been! Not worrying about having to impress God, not worrying about things they had to accomplish, they could utilize all their energies in simply enjoying God. God had already completed everything necessary for their happiness. It was up to them now to experience it, to relish it, to revel in it.

So right here, in the very beginning of human history, God is making a very significant theological statement that works itself out in a vital spiritual experience—both symbolized by the Sabbath rest: We cannot justify ourselves, we cannot achieve God's state of perfect rest by our own efforts, we cannot trust in our own abilities, we simply accept what God offers us as a gift of divine grace. The Sabbath is a perpetual reminder for us to look away from ourselves and our endeavors and to look to God and His endeavors.

The eminent theologian, Karl Barth, concurs:

> God's rest day is man's first day. Hence man's life be-
> gins with the gospel, not the law, in freedom to celebrate with
> joy the festal day of God, not with an obligation laid upon
> him to perform some task, to labor and toil. Man rests before
> he works.[4]

A second implication of what it means to enter into God's Sabbath rest by resting from our works is to always conceive of the Sabbath as the first day in our relationship to God. God met Adam and
Eve on their first full day with the gift of His rest—an opportunity to
enjoy intimate fellowship with Him. Humanity's history with God
thus begins on the Sabbath, the seventh day of Creation week, not the
first.

Consequently, as Dr. Kubo points out, the significant experiential reality should be that God must come first in our lives, in our
thought, in our planning. Only as we come to God before we do anything else, before we begin the workweek, will we have our priorities
in the right order. Only then will we know how to put the rest of the
week in the proper perspective.[5] Entering into God's Sabbath rest
systematically and regularly helps to remind us of this important spiritual principle: God comes first. When that becomes the truth around
which every aspect of our lives revolve, the fires of spiritual renewal
cannot be extinguished. As Jesus said, "Seek first his kingdom and
his righteousness, and all these things will be given to you as well"
(Matthew 6:33, NIV).

Here Jesus is talking about where we choose to put our trust.
Will it be in material possessions, in our attempts at survival, in our
concerns for food and clothing? Or will we choose to trust in God
and His power and promise to provide? Will we choose to place spiritual realities ("his kingdom and his righteousness") in precedence
over physical realities ("what shall we eat" or "what shall we drink"

or "what shall we wear?")?

Wasn't this picture of priorities what Jesus had in mind in John 6:27 when, after having miraculously multiplied the bread and fish, He said to the crowds who had followed Him to the other side of Lake Galilee, " 'Do not work for food that spoils, but for food that endures to eternal life, which the Son of Man will give you.' "

Again, the apostle Paul, in 2 Corinthians 4:18, reiterates this important spiritual principle: "We fix our eyes not on what is seen, but on what is unseen. For what is seen is temporary, but what is unseen is eternal."

A statement from the Palestinian Talmud puts this priority in perspective: "Man was created on the eve of the Sabbath in order that he might begin life by a religious practice."[6]

So the Sabbath calls us, reminds us, that for life to fulfill its original purpose and meaning, God must be first in everything. Life begins and ends with grace, not merit. That was God's design from the very beginning of time. For this reason He gives us the Sabbath rest and graciously invites us to enter into it.

Karl Barth summarizes it this way:

> The aim of the Sabbath commandment is that man shall give and allow the omnipotent grace of God to have the first and last word at every point; that he shall surrender to it completely, in the least as well as in the greatest things; that he shall place himself, with his knowing, willing and doing, unconditionally at His disposal. It aims at this complete surrender and capitulation by singling out one day, the seventh, and thus the seventh part of the whole lifetime of every man, from the succession of his work days, by forbidding him to make this day another work day, and by bidding him place himself on this day directly as it were in relation to the omnipotence [sic] grace of God and under its control.[7]

Entering into God's Sabbath rest, a vacation with God—basking in the sunlight of God's grace, the warmth of His acceptance and approval, not because of what we have done or accomplished but for what He has done and completed. Grace from beginning to end. It is God's activity that is important, not ours. This is where the Sabbath rest begins.

Central to this "rest of grace," as Ellen White calls it,[8] is the beautiful picture of God putting as His priority His friendship with humanity. On this seventh day of Creation, this Sabbath rest, God the Creator approaches Adam and Eve as their Friend, One who loves them, not as they should be but as they are.

Have you ever watched an adult who really loves a child try to talk to that child? What does the adult do? The adult bends down or squats to get eye level with the child. Why? Getting on the same level helps "to guarantee laughter and love without intimidation," suggests Karen Burton Mains.[9] Friendship is easier that way, being on the same level.

This is what the Sabbath pictures: God bending down to us in order to relate to us on our level—whatever it takes for us not to be afraid to be His friends.

This Sabbath rest of grace is the antithesis of fear. God isn't into intimidation. Grace never produces fear. Rather, it draws and beckons, renews and revives. What produces fear is legalism.

As Manning says, legalism "is a religious response to human fear. What makes legalism so attractive is that it meets a basic human need—security."[10] What provides spiritual security for the legalist? Security is all the things that are being accomplished and achieved for God, a checklist religion—something tangible to ascertain one's progress.

But if we believe our acceptance with God is based on accomplishments, there remains the nagging worry that there might possibly be something left undone that needs to be done—some behavior off the list that needs to be put on (not to mention the fact that one might fail in fulfilling the list). Should there be failure, God's acceptance would no longer be secured. Punishment would have to follow. That's the attitude of the legalist.

Isn't this the reason Adam and Eve, when they first ate the fruit, suddenly became afraid of God (Gen. 3:8-13)? They knew they had disobeyed Him, and since they had been led to believe by the serpent that God's love and acceptance were based upon performance, not upon grace (vv. 4-6), they were afraid of His anger and punishment.

So what did they do when they heard God's voice calling them to fellowship? They hid from Him—"Maybe He'll think we're not home and leave when He doesn't find us here!" They covered themselves with leaves—"Maybe He'll think we're just trees and leave." Fear never leads to fellowship, it always leads to isolation.

For this reason, God begins human history with His rest—Sabbath—a vacation with Him—His continual reassurance that His love and acceptance of us are rooted and grounded in His grace, not our works.

In a captivating phrase, Roy Branson states, "The Sabbath is God's weekly 'Yes' to humanity."[11] As Bacchiocchi puts it, it is "God's assurance of His constant availability, . . . that He is listening and responding, that He wants dialogue and fellowship" no matter what, no strings attached.[12] That is Good News!

But it isn't good news to legalists! This divine generosity is a scandal to them. It upsets their basis for security, and they fight against it. They just don't understand it.

In one of his plays, Jean Anouilh portrays the *Last Judgment* as he imagines it: The just are densely clustered at the gate of heaven eager to march in, sure of their reserved seats and bursting with impatience. Suddenly a rumor starts spreading. They look at one another in disbelief. "Look, He's going to forgive those others too." They gasp and sputter: "After all the trouble I went through. I just can't believe it."

Exasperated, they work themselves into a fury and start cursing

God, and at that very instant, they are damned. That was the final judgment. They judged themselves, excommunicated themselves. Love appeared, and they refused to acknowledge it. "We don't approve of a heaven that's open to every Tom, Dick, and Harry. We spurn this God who lets everyone off. We can't love a God who loves so foolishly."[13]

The legalist, confronted with this God of *grace,* lives a life of fear, lack of assurance, and no peace, because he knows that God does the unexpected, springs surprises, since He can't be absolutized and pigeonholed. To cover up his insecurities, he judges and condemns. It's a terrible way to exist.

Jesus knows that. So He continues to affirm and invite: " 'Come to me, all you who are weary and burdened, and I will give you rest. Take my yoke upon you and learn from me, for I am gentle and humble in heart, and you will find rest for your souls. For my yoke is easy and my burden is light' " (Matt. 11:28-30). Rest! Real rest!

The Sabbath rest of grace. What an invitation!

God's love is based on nothing, and the fact that it is based on nothing makes us secure. Were it based on anything we do, and that "anything" were to collapse, then God's love would crumble as well. But with the God of Jesus no such thing can possibly happen. People who realize this can live freely and to the full. Remember Atlas, who carries the whole world? We have Christian Atlases who mistakenly carry the burden of trying to deserve God's love. Even the mere watching of this lifestyle is depressing. I'd like to say to Atlas: "Put that globe down and dance on it. That's why God made it." And to these weary Christian Atlases: "Lay down your load and build your life on God's love." We don't have to earn this love; neither do we have to support it. It is a free gift.[14]

God's Sabbath rest of grace is a regular reminder for us to rest from our works and attempts to justify ourselves before Him, to stop trying to earn His acceptance. He loves and accepts us as we are, not as we should be. That's grace!

So the Sabbath is a celebration of God's rhythm of time: rest and work, night and day, grace and law—in those orders. Every time we celebrate the Sabbath, we reenter that sequence. We remember what comes first. The more we celebrate it on Sabbath, the easier it becomes to remember it during the week.

One of the ways we're continually reminded of this sequence is not only every Sabbath but also every day: God designed the Hebrew evening/morning sequence to condition us to the rhythms of grace. Here's how Eugene Peterson describes it. He says that when we go to sleep, God begins His work. As we sleep, God develops His covenant. When we wake up, we're called out to participate in God's creative action. We respond in faith, in work. But always grace is previous. Grace is primary. We wake into a world we didn't make, into a salvation we didn't earn.

Evening: God begins, without our help, His creative day. Morning: God calls us to enjoy and share and develop the work He initiated. Creation and covenant are sheer grace and there to greet us every morning. George MacDonald calls sleep God's contrivance for giving us the help He cannot get into us when we are awake.[15]

Evening and morning sequence, Sabbath rest, God's rhythm of grace, are tools given us to help us stay out of the way so God can really act.

The Call to Worship had just been pronounced starting Easter Sunday morning service in an East Texas church. The choir started its processional singing "Up From the Grave He Arose" as they marched in perfect step down the center aisle to the front of the church.

The last lady in the choir was wearing shoes with very slender heels. Without a thought for her fancy heels, she marched toward the grating that covered the hot air register in the middle of the aisle. Suddenly the heel of one shoe sank into the hole in the register grate. Immediately she realized her predicament. Not wanting to hold up the whole processional and make a big scene, without missing a step, she slipped her foot out of her shoe and continued marching down the aisle. There wasn't a hitch. The processional moved with clocklike precision. She felt so good!

The first man after her spotted the situation and without losing a step himself, reached down and pulled up her shoe. Unfortunately, the entire grate came with it! Surprised, but still singing, the man kept on going down the aisle, holding in his hand the grate with the shoe attached. Everything still moved like clockwork, though. The man and woman had done well, in spite of the odds.

Still in tune, still in step, the next man in line, not seeing what had happened in front of him, stepped right into the open register and suddenly disappeared from sight. The service took on a special meaning that Sunday, for just as the choir ended with "Allelujah! Christ Arose!" a voice was heard under the church shouting, "I hope all of you are out of the way 'cause I'm coming out now!"

With eyes as wide as silver dollars, the little girl closest to the aisle shouted out, "Come on up, Jesus! We'll stay out of the way!"[16]

"Come on up, Jesus! We'll stay out of the way!" That's what the Sabbath rest is all about—a willingness to stay out of the way, to rest from our feeble attempts to control life, to earn God's favor, and simply to let His grace wash over us like waves on the sandy beach. This is the Sabbath rest of grace—vacationing with God.

The golfer, Arnold Palmer, once played a series of exhibition matches in Saudi Arabia. The king was so impressed that he proposed to give Palmer a gift. Out of a mixture of embarrassment and desire to be scrupulous, Palmer declined, saying, "It really isn't necessary, Your Highness. I'm honored simply to have been invited here."

The king pushed his offer: "I would be deeply upset if you would not allow me to give you a gift!"

Palmer thought for a moment, wondering what small, insignificant thing he could ask for that would look appropriate and still satisfy the king's interest.

"All right," he said, "how about a golf club? That would be a beautiful memento of my visit to your country." He would be happy to receive a putter or pitching wedge, even if they were gold-plated.

The next day, delivered to Palmer's hotel, was the title deed to a golf club. Thousands of acres, trees, lakes, clubhouse. . . .[17]

We're so often content with so little when God wants to give us so much! As Manning comments, "Don't order 'just a piece of toast' when eggs Benedict are on the menu. Don't come with a thimble when God has nothing less to give you than the ocean of Himself." Don't be contented with a "nice day" when Jesus says, "It has pleased My Father to give you the Kingdom."[18]

God wants to give us rest, His love and acceptance, His whole kingdom, for free—we insist on paying for it! He wants to give us vacation time with Him—we insist on working. He wants to be our Friend—we insist on being slaves.

It's so true, isn't it—most of us are too often too busy trying frenetically to accomplish and achieve, calling it a *mission* for God, that we miss our *vacation* with God, "wasting" time doing nothing around Him, just enjoying Him. Without the gift of Sabbath rest, in which we rest from our "works," spiritual renewal will never take place because we'll simply be too busy. No wonder God didn't merely suggest the Sabbath in the beginning, He commanded it (Exodus 20:8-11)—"for nothing less than a command has the power to intervene in the vicious, accelerating, self-perpetuating cycle of faithless and graceless busyness."[19]

So in reality, far from being a legalistic demand, God's commandment is an act of grace to help us experience a God of grace. For spiritual renewal, we must learn to enter into Sabbath rest, to get out of the way, to rest from our works and simply vacaion with God. But as will now become clear, this resting from our works is for a significant purpose: We rest *from* our works in order to rest *in* God's work.

Chapter 6

Resting in God's Work

Karen Burton Mains draws from nature to illustrate the issues surrounding this important spiritual principle. She describes the predicament of the jungle along the Amazon River Basin in Brazil with the tragic deforestation that is going on.

A study, headed by Eneas Salati of the University of Sao Paulo in Brazil, shows that forested land returns ten times the moisture to the atmosphere as deforested land and produces 50 percent of the rain that falls on it. According to the research, cutting down the tropical rain forests reduces rainfall and increases temperature. These findings are being seen by experts to have serious implications for global weather patterns.

Even so, says Mains, our spiritual world is being ravaged, defoliated, deforested. "We have become a dehydrated people, with meager supernatural life, dwelling in desert places of the soul. God meant what He said, 'Remember the Sabbath day to keep it holy' (Exod. 20:8)."[1]

Without regular, systematic spiritual rehydration, the fountain of the Spirit within our souls will never flow freely, our spiritual growth will be stunted, and we will be unable to become the kind of people God wants us to be. As Ahva J. C. Bond says, "Six days of labor will feed and clothe the body; Sabbath labor will starve the soul."[2] In other words, disregard the Sabbath rest and reap the consequences of spiritual dehydration.

For that reason, one author writes, "Without [the Sabbath], man cannot realize the spiritual potential that is his. With it he finds a relationship that far exceeds his spiritual expectations."[3]

So God graciously gives us the Sabbath, a day to rest from our works of human achievements in order to rest in God's works of salvation for us, to rest in His power to restore our souls, to tenderize our spirits, to harmonize our hearts with His.

The question is, how does this work? How is it that the Sabbath rest can do this for our spirituality? How can resting in God's works bring about spiritual renewal?

Paul Tillich, in his book *Dynamics of Faith,* suggests a significant concept in his discussion about symbols. He explains that a symbol not only opens up dimensions and elements of reality that otherwise would remain unapproachable but also unlocks dimensions and elements of our soul that correspond to the dimensions and elements of reality. "There are within us dimensions of which we cannot become aware except through symbols, as melodies and rhythms in music."[4]

This is why the arts, such as music, drama, art, writing, play such a significant role in opening up new vistas of thought and emotion that ultimately lead to new behaviors. Utilizing the right side of the brain, which is stimulated by the arts and which deals with abstract thinking, brings into consciousness previously unseen connections and relationships between ideas and concepts.

It's been found by some, for example, that the ability to write and convey concepts can be enhanced by listening to quiet music in the background. Working the right side of the brain stimulates creativity. The power of music and art is astounding, and yet how few people avail themselves of such opportunities.

Tillich goes on to say that "a symbol participates in the reality for which it stands."[5] In other words, by experiencing the symbol, one can experience what the symbol stands for.

Tillich uses the flag of a country to illustrate how this works. The flag of the United States, for example, participates in the power and dignity of our nation for which it stands. That's why an attack on the flag is felt by so many Americans as an attack on themselves. Isn't this why the flag-burning issue evoked such passion in this country a few years ago?

I've noticed that when I watch on TV rebels in other countries burning and stomping on the effigy of Uncle Sam, a feeling of anger develops inside. "How dare they do that to the symbol of my government!"

Why do we feel these emotions? After all, why should a dumb mannequin mean anything, anyway? Uncle Sam isn't a real uncle. Why should we care? Because the symbol participates in the reality to which it points. And when we recognize and accept the symbol, we experience the reality for which it stands. As Fritz Guy says, "The meaning and the experience of the symbol are inseparable in actuality."[6]

Guy points out that central to the Sabbath are the dual concepts of the "relatedness and ultimacy of God," the truth that God is both close to us and far beyond us, both approachable and unreachable, understandable and unfathomable, revealed and hidden. So the Sabbath both points to these qualities of God and is a means by which we can experience them.[7]

Notice, for example, Ellen White's comments along this line:

To those who reverence His holy day the Sabbath is a sign that God recognizes them as His chosen people. It is *a pledge that He will fulfill to them His covenant.* Every soul who accepts this sign of God's government places himself under the divine, everlasting covenant. He fastens Himself to the golden chain of obedience, *every link of which is a promise.*"[8]

What does this say about the Sabbath? By participating in God's Sabbath, the symbol of His rest, we experience the reality to which that rest points. Entering into the symbol of God's Sabbath rest, choosing to vacation with God, can enhance spirituality in two ways.

First, by a willingness to respect God's rhythm of time by entering into His Sabbath rest, we place ourselves within an atmosphere that facilitates a deeper appreciation in our hearts and minds of the spiritual side of life. This takes place as we immerse ourselves in the realm of symbols, like we do on Friday nights when we gather around the supper table and light the Sabbath candles; when we sit together as a family and have worship and sing and read stories; when we come to church and participate in all the symbols of worship like music, prayer, stories, offerings, foot-washing, and Communion; when we have a special menu for Sabbath meals; when we gather with friends; go to the park or on a walk; etc. Experiencing all these develops within us the ability to be more sensitive to spiritual issues. We're giving the right side of our brains opportunity to expand to a greater degree. Appreciation for spirituality is heightened by this intentional atmosphere.

Second, by a willingness to respect God's rhythm of time by entering into His Sabbath rest, we confirm to Him that we honor, love, and respect Him, that we're willing to abide by our covenant with Him. By placing ourselves in that covenant relationship with Him, we're entitled to all the promises of the covenant, not the least of which is His promise to make us holy as He is holy:

"Also I gave them my Sabbaths as a sign between us, so they would know that I the LORD made them holy" (Ezekiel 20:12); "You must observe my Sabbaths. This will be a sign between me and you for the generations to come, so you may know that I am the LORD, who makes you holy. Observe the Sabbath, because it is holy to you. . . . The seventh day is a Sabbath of rest, holy to the LORD" (Exodus 31:13-15).

Notice that in these texts, the concept of holiness *of* time is connected with holiness *in* time. This suggests that the blessing of holiness, sanctification, is promised through the Sabbath rest. Entering into the holiness of time carries with it the potential of experiencing holiness in time. How does this work?

According to an ancient Jewish tradition, "The Sabbath possesses a holiness like that of the world to come."[9] In what way? Rabbi Heschel enlarges the thought by noting that the idea of the Sabbath as a queen or a bride is not a personification of the Sabbath but "an exemplification of a divine attribute, an illustration of God's need for human love; it does not represent a substance but the presence of God, His relationship to man."[10]

What makes the Sabbath time holy is God's presence. When God rested on the seventh day of Creation, it means He did more than merely stop His work of creation because it was all finished. It was not a negation of activity. Rather, it was a change of activity. He blessed the Sabbath day and made it holy (Exod. 20:11). In other words, "He filled it with His presence."[11] That was His final creative act in Creation week.

Bacchiocchi shows how the Sabbath can heighten holiness by pointing out that on the Sabbath, Moses "entered into the cloud" (Exod. 24:18) of God's personal presence and received both "the tables of stone, with the law and the commandment" (Exod. 24:12)—a revelation of God's principles of conduct—and the pattern of the tabernacle (Exod. 25:9)—God's provisions for atonement and worship. In other words, "The Sabbath is the day when God both communicates a knowledge of His will and grants His grace to implement it."[12]

What's the result? As Karl Barth states, "In the completion of His work, He entered into a free and living fellowship with man, and brought man into fellowship with Himself. Only when this had been achieved could man set off into the week."[13]

In other words, holiness in time comes as a result of fellowship with a holy God. That's why God, in an act of grace, commands us to keep the Sabbath. It's a regular opportunity to fellowship with, to "rub shoulders" with, a holy God.

In a special way on Sabbath we may put aside our daily work and participate in deep personal communion with the Holy One of Israel, and in that intimate relationship become changed more and more into His likeness. . . . He knows that this sanctifying personal relationship is vital to our spiritual growth and development.[14]

In the same way, author Clifford Hansen asserts that not only is the Sabbath a symbol of our spiritual rest in God, it's also a means for attaining it. "The Sabbath . . . provides the time so essential for that spiritual culture which will build these ideals into human life."[15]

So, how does entering into God's Sabbath rest renew our spirituality? It provides regular blocks of time to experience intimate fellowship with a holy God who's promised that by reflecting upon and contemplating His glory, we "are being transformed into His likeness with ever-increasing glory, which comes from the Lord, who is the Spirit" (2 Corinthians 3:18). The presence of God provides the power of God—the habitation of God holds out the holiness of God.

So vacationing with God is entering into God's Sabbath rest by resting from our works in order to rest in His works—"so they would know that I the Lord made them holy" (Ezek. 20:12).

Notice what the apostle Paul says in Ephesians 2:10. After stressing the truth that we're saved purely through God's grace, if we're willing to accept it as a gift ("through faith"), he writes: "We are God's workmanship, created in Christ Jesus to do good works, which God prepared in advance for us to do." The allusion to creation is significant. The "good works" for us to do have been created/prepared "in advance."

By the time Adam and Eve were created, God had already finished preparing everything necessary for their lives. All that remained for them at that point was their willingness to accept His gifts, to rest in them, to use them for His glory, to spend time in fellowship with Him. So God provides, for their first full day, the Sabbath rest, a day for them to rest from their own works in order to rest in His already prepared works for them, to enjoy Him and all that He has made for them.

Later on, in Ephesians 4:24, Paul reemphasizes, "put on the new self, created to be like God in true righteousness and holiness." Again the allusion to creation is significant. Righteousness and holiness are acts of creation by God that we willingly accept as gifts and incorporate into our lives. Entering God's Sabbath rest, therefore, is a demonstration of our desire to be like God, to accept His righteousness and holiness He offers to us in fellowship with Him.

The prophet Isaiah captures both the essence and the celebration of this experience: "I delight greatly in the LORD; my soul rejoices in my God. For He has clothed me with garments of salvation and arrayed me in a robe of righteousness, as a bridegroom adorns his head like a priest, and as a bride adorns herself with her jewels" (Isaiah 61:10).

Matitiahu Tsevat, a scholar of the Hebrew Scriptures, insists that the basic meaning of the biblical Sabbath is an "acceptance of the sovereignty of God . . . [that] reminds us that God is the master of time" in which we renounce our autonomy and affirm God's dominion over us.[16] By entering into God's Sabbath rest, we are showing our desire to belong to Him as our Savior and Lord.

Sanctification, our daily acknowledgment of God's sovereignty over us, the choice to let God be God in our lives, our daily choosing to rest in His gift of holiness and righteousness, is so often a difficult process. We battle the desire for self-mastery and self-dominion. We fall into the trap of thinking our works are better than God's. We often fail. So the risk of self-delusion and the temptation to give up are always there.

This is another reason why the Sabbath is so important for our spiritual growth and renewal. One of the significant aspects of resting from our own works to rest in God's works is the regular recognition that not only is God the One who does the work in us, He's also a God of completion. The Sabbath is not only a day to remember Creation, it is also a day "that rejoices in the completion of the creation. It is God the completer, the finisher, who rejoices in the Sabbath rest, the day of perfection."[17]

God's Sabbath rest is a rest in His completed work. Genesis 2:2 describes it, "By the seventh day God had finished the work He had been doing; so on the seventh day He rested from all his work." The reason for God's command not to work on the Sabbath (Exod. 20:11; 31:14-17) is because the Sabbath is a celebration of God's completed work. There's no more to be done—He has finished His work. Our working on that day would be to deny God's completed work, implying that our work is more important than His.

What are the spiritual implications for us? Ottilie Stafford concludes: "It is the day which promises . . . a completion of all that is incomplete in our lives."[18] God always finishes what He starts. So Paul encourages us with his words, "Being confident of this, that he who began a good work in you will carry it on to completion until the day of Christ Jesus" (Philippians 1:6). The author of Hebrews also writes, "Let us fix our eyes on Jesus, the author and perfecter of our faith" (Heb. 12:2). Earlier, he encourages with the counsel, "Let us hold unswervingly to the hope we profess, for he who promised is faithful" (10:23).

In fact, in the very chapter in which the author of Hebrews talks about the Sabbath rest, admonishing the believers to make every effort to enter into it, he concludes by saying, "Let us then approach the throne of grace with confidence, so that we may receive mercy and find grace to help us in our time of need" (4:16). If God promises to do something for us (like making us holy), He will do it and not stop until the job is finished. That's what the Sabbath rest reminds us of.

Richard Davidson captures the beauty of this truth as he graphically illustrates the Sabbath rest described in the Psalms' love song for the Sabbath, Psalm 92, especially verses 10-12. Notice the delightful images of the abundant life promised by God through the Sabbath in this section:

The exalted horn—rejoice in this biblical symbol of defensive and offensive power and victory in the Christian life. Let it sink in—*God* does the exalting; He takes responsibility for your success. *The wild ox (or ibex)*—picture your God-given freedom from all tyranny of time and schedule. Assimilate the divine promise in the psalmist's striking imagery—poise and gracefulness like the ibex bounding over the mountaintops. Experience the calmness that fills the life of the person who knows the Lord of the Sabbath. As you cling to the strength of such a God, no amount of trouble or turmoil can destroy you.

The fine oil—feel the soothing and healing balm poured upon your wounds in life. Sense the refreshing of the Spirit as He energizes and fills you with enthusiasm. The defeat of your adversaries—taste the joy of *present* victory over spiritual foes, as well as past deliverance and future assurance of conquest.

Experience the growth, the flourishing, not like the grass that soon withers, but like *the date palm*—called by the inhabitants of the Near East a "blessed tree, the sister of man." See its perennial green foliage, its vital force constantly renewing itself from its roots. Its diadem of leaves—grasp the symbol of your victory and royalty in Christ. Behold its fruit, more than 600 pounds of yield in a single season. Bask in the usefulness and productivity God promises for your future.

Gaze at *the mighty cedar of Lebanon*—prince among the trees of the mountains, graceful, with lofty growth. Sense its year-round greenness and the pleasant perfume of its needles, and visualize the freshness and fragrance of life that is yours. Claim the promised strength and nobility symbolized by the cedar of Lebanon.

In short, this section of Psalm 92 tells us to absorb the meaning of the Sabbath; *it is a promise of the abundant and victorious life.* Thus it is the sign of sanctification.[19]

So the Sabbath rest celebrates God the completer, the finisher, who refuses to stop until the work is done and perfected. "Stronger than the energy of light, which silently creates the flower from the seed, is the creative influence of God's wish for us."[20]

What a promise to remember, not just weekly but daily, in those moments when failure and frustration dog our steps. Resting in God's works means resting in the promise that God will bring to completion His work of sanctification in our lives if we'll just let Him be God. A holy God in holy time creating a holy people—that's the Good News of the Sabbath rest.

This is why a Hollywood movie like "City of Angels" is so incomplete in its solution to our human predicament. It says that for us to experience real life, we must choose earth over eternity. But the Sabbath reminds us that that is, in fact, a false choice. The Sabbath reveals to us that choosing eternity in God now is to choose real life, real pleasure, real fulfillment. Only in Him can we experience abundant living.

In an article titled "The Man Who Planted Trees and Grew Happiness," published in *Friends of Nature*, Jean Giono tells the story of Elzeard Bouffier, a shepherd he met in 1913 in mountain heights unknown to tourists in a region of the French Alps.[21] At this time the area was a barren and colorless land where nothing grew but wild lavender. Former villages were now desolate, springs had run dry, and over this high unsheltered land, the wind blew with unendurable ferocity.

While mountain climbing, Giono began searching for water and came to a shepherd's hut into which he was invited for a meal and to spend the night. Giono tells of his host's evening activity after the simple dinner.

The shepherd went to fetch a small sack and poured out a heap of acorns on the table. He began inspecting them, one by one, with great concentration, separating the good from the bad. When he had set aside a large enough pile of good acorns, he counted them out by tens, meanwhile eliminating the small ones or those that were slightly cracked, for now he examined them more closely. When he had selected one hundred perfect acorns, he stopped and went to bed.

Giono discovered that the shepherd had been planting trees on the wild hillsides. In three years he had planted 100,000, of which 20,000 had sprouted. Of the 20,000, the quiet man expected to lose half to rodents or to the harshness of alpine nature. There remained 10,000 oak trees to grow where nothing had grown before.

At this time in his life, Elzeard Bouffier was fifty-five years old. But he said his work was just beginning. Giono informed him that in thirty years his 10,000 oaks would be magnificent. The shepherd answered simply that if God granted him life, in thirty years he would have planted so many more that the 10,000 would be insignificant.

Returning to the mountainside after World War I, Giono discovered an incredible forest and a chain-reaction in creation. The desolation was giving way to wild growth, water flowed in the once empty brooks. The wind scattered seeds, and the ecology, sheltered by a leafy roof and bonded to the earth by a mat of spreading roots, became hospitable. Willows, rushes, meadows, gardens, flowers were born. The once desolate villages were reinhabited.

Government forestry officials came to admire this reforestation. A natural forest, they exclaimed, had sprung up spontaneously, none of them suspecting the precision and dedication of so exceptional a personality as the tree-planter who worked in total solitude, without need for human recognition. Giono shared his knowledge of Bouffier's work with one forestry officer, "a man who knew how to keep silent."

Commenting on Bouffier's health at age seventy-five, Giono writes:

> In the direction from which we had come the slopes were covered with trees twenty to twenty-five feet tall. I remembered how the land had looked in 1913: a desert . . . Peaceful, regular toil; the vigorous mountain air; frugality and, above all, serenity in the spirit had endowed this old man with awe-inspiring health. He was one of God's athletes. I wondered how many more acres he was going to cover with trees.

Giono returned again to the region after World War II. Thirty kilometers away from the war lines, the simple shepherd had quietly and peacefully continued his work, ignoring the war of 1939 like he had the war of 1914. The reformation of the land had continued. Eight years later the whole countryside glowed with health and prosperity.

On the site of the ruins seen in 1913 now stand neat farms. The old streams, fed by the rains and snows that the forest conserves, are flowing again. Little by little the villages have been rebuilt. People from the plains, where land is costly, have settled here, bringing youth, motion, and the spirit of adventure. Along the roads you meet hearty men and women, boys and girls who understand laughter and have recovered a taste for picnics. Counting the former population, unrecognizable now that they live in comfort, more than 10,000 people owe their happiness to Elzeard Bouffier.

What an incredible illustration of what God wants to do in the lives of His people! That's the Good News of the Sabbath rest, our vacation with God—like the simple shepherd did to that desolate mountainside, God offers us renewal. He wants to reforest the stripped and barren waste places of our souls, to restore our spiritual ecology "until the sacred blooms, takes hold, spreads, leafs, shelters."[22] He refuses to quit until the job is done. That's the Good News of God's Sabbath rest!

Sabbath rest and spiritual renewal—a resting from our works (justification) and a resting in God's works (sanctification): both experiences center around the word *rest*. In summarizing this section, then, it might be helpful to note that the Hebrew word for rest, *menuha,* obviously means more than a withdrawal from labor and exertion, more than merely a cessation of activity. As Rabbi Heschel points out, to the biblical mind *menuha* is the same as happiness and stillness, peace and harmony. He makes a fascinating connection between this word for Sabbath rest and the essence of the good life described in Psalm 23 which uses the same word—"beside still waters" (v. 2—"waters of *menuhot*").[23]

With that connection between the Sabbath rest and Psalm 23, notice how the Sabbath rest is described in the psalm, the qualities and promised experiences being offered by God to those willing to enter in. What a fitting summary to this section:

> The LORD is my shepherd, I shall not be in want. He makes me lie down in green pastures, he leads me beside quiet waters, he restores my soul. He guides me in paths of righteousness for his name's sake. Even though I walk through the valley of the shadow of death, I will fear no evil, for you are with me; your rod and your staff, they comfort me.
>
> You prepare a table before me in the presence of my enemies. You anoint my head with oil; my cup overflows. Surely goodness and love will follow me all the days of my

life, and I will dwell in the house of the Lord forever.

This is the Good News of the Sabbath rest—God's free offer for spiritual renewal to rekindle the fire of the Spirit's passion within, to extend to us a level and depth of fellowship and friendship with Him unsurpassed by anything this world tries to offer, a vacation with God—good news indeed!

Chapter 7

Falling in Love With God All Over Again

Have you ever looked at a simple drop of water through a microscope? The view is amazing! I remember as a child finally getting the microscope I had wanted for so long! What an excitement it was to place things on a slide and look at them up close. I'll never forget looking at that first drop of water under the microscope. What a whole new world! All kinds of life forms and things swimming and moving around. I said to myself, "And we drink this stuff?"

It is an amazing view! Things invisible to our eyes can suddenly be seen in that simple drop of water. Something so common, so ordinary takes on a whole new perspective when seen through a different lens.

The same is true of spiritual truth; sometimes the most familiar truths often need to be examined through a different lens in order to be appreciated for their full significance.

Like the Sabbath, for instance. The holy, awesome implications of Sabbath have been lost to so many Christians, including many Adventists, because we have been looking at it from one lens only:

which day is the right day.

But the Bible provides another lens, an incredible motif that weaves and winds its way through the stories of Scripture, that gives a perspective that has the potential of radically transforming our experience of God through the Sabbath. What is that lens that has fallen into such neglect? It is the progressive theme of the Divine Romance. Unless the Sabbath is viewed through this lens, it cannot be understood and experienced the way God has intended it to be.[1]

The Divine Romance

Have you ever seen or read the play by Tennessee Williams, *The Glass Menagerie*? The main characters are from one family, the Wingfields. There's mother Amanda, who clings frantically to a lost time in her past; there's daughter Laura, a crippled young woman of frail beauty who has failed to establish contact with reality and lives in a make-believe world centering around her fragile collection of miniature glass animals; and then there's son Tom who is restless with his life and often resents the responsibility and burden of having to take care of these two dependents weighing heavily on his shoulders.

What heats up this drama is mother Amanda's continual insistence that her son, Tom, should bring home some work acquaintance to be a gentleman caller for her painfully shy and withdrawn Laura. After all, every woman needs a gentleman caller, she insists . . . and then mother Amanda gives her regular speech about her glorious past:

> Why one Sunday afternoon in the Blue Mountains—your mother received—seventeen!—that's right, seventeen!—gentlemen callers! . . . And my callers were gentlemen all right! Some of the most prominent young planters of the Mississippi Delta—planters and sons of planters! . . . And then there was that boy that every girl in the Delta had set her heart for! That beautiful, brilliant young Fitzhugh boy from Greene County![2]

The last part of the play shows the coming of a real gentleman caller, a wonderfully nice young man named Jim O'Connor who is, for the most part, unaware of Laura and who, unbeknownst to Tom and Amanda, is engaged to another young woman. But before this fact is revealed, there's a scene of exquisite tenderness in the Wingfields' apartment: After a lavishly prepared dinner which stretches the Wingfield family's already meager means, Jim kindly focuses his attention on Laura. Alone in the living room while Tom and his mother are doing the dishes in the kitchen, Jim sees in Laura a particular uniqueness. Lightheartedly, he asks her to dance with him to the music floating up the narrow alley from the Paradise Dance Hall, across the murky canyons of tangled clotheslines, garbage cans, and crisscrossed fire escapes.

Laura is so shy and timid she protests. Besides, how can she dance with one foot shorter than the other and an awkward brace on that leg? But Jim literally sweeps her around the room for a brief, happy moment. Suddenly, they bump into a table, and the unicorn, Laura's favorite glass horse in her glass menagerie, falls to the floor and breaks into pieces. Jim apologizes, not knowing how important this glass horse is to Laura. As he watches her pick up the glass pieces in her hand, he notices her own delicate, glasslike quality in the soft glow of the candlelight and says:

> Has anyone ever told you that you were pretty? Well, you are! In a very different way from anyone else. And all the nicer because of the difference, too . . . I wish that you were my sister. I'd teach you to have some confidence in yourself. The different people aren't like other people, but being different is nothing to be ashamed of. Because other people aren't such wonderful people. They're one hundred times one thousand. You're one times one! They walk all over the earth. You just stay here. They're common as—weeds, but—you—well you're—Blue Roses![3]

Laura blushes. She had known and admired Jim from a distance six years before when he was the high school hero, the basketball star, captain of the debating club, president of the senior class and the glee club, and the male singing lead in the annual light operas. She had sat across the aisle from him in the auditorium on Mondays, Wednesdays, and Fridays. And once, when she had been absent, he had asked her what the matter was. When she answered that she had been sick from pleurosis, Jim thought she said blue roses and that became his nickname for her through high school, his special name for her shy, unobtrusive self—Blue Roses.

The God who comes close

This is the kind of stuff that weaves and winds its way through the stories of the Divine Romance. Karen Burton Mains pictures the poignant comparison: Like handsome Jim, gallant and lighthearted, who leans in concern across the auditorium aisle, God leans close and calls us by our special name. He calls us when, like Laura, crippled and disfigured, we clump awkwardly with our metal brace up the stairs, the noise embarrassing, sounding like thunder to our own ears; and He calls that endearing name as we, like Laura, hide among the frail toys we allow to occupy us because we're too timid to face the realities and competitions of a harsh world. He showers us with flattering attentions. We blush, amazed to be suddenly the focus of His gaze. He watches us—jealously even—and moves perceptibly closer when others are near. This is the picture of God, the ultimate Gentleman Caller, the lover of our souls who woos and courts each of us as though we're the only one.[4]

The dramatization of this Divine Romance begins early in scripture. Exodus 6:6, 7: "I am the LORD, and . . . I will take you as my own people, and I will be your God." Who are these words spoken to? To Israel, a slave girl of Egypt, under hard bondage, misused, abused, forlorn—but now suddenly favored, because the eye of a powerful Lord has noticed her, sees her potential beauty, and is determined to set her free. It's as though He has said, "I will be your man, and you will be my woman."

What happens next? He plans an incredibly daring rescue for this slave maiden called Israel! He executes a heroic master plan, involving escape at night, chase in the dark, what looks like doom, and then a last-minute deliverance at the Red Sea at dawn. Moses wrote a song about it—Exodus 15:1,13—" 'I will sing to the LORD, for he is highly exalted. The horse and its rider he has hurled into the sea. . . . In your unfailing love you will lead the people you have redeemed.' "

Sir Walter Scott captured the essence of breathless last-minute deliverance in his romantic story *Ivanhoe*.[4] The beautiful Jewess woman named Rebecca has been nursing the wounded and disinherited Lord Wilfred of Ivanhoe back to health. It's a slow process for him to get well again. During his time of recovery, while she tenderly cares for him, she falls in love with him, secretly, though, because she knows there is no hope since she's a Jew. Her heart aches inside.

One day she's kidnapped from Ivanhoe's surroundings by the self-centered Templar Knight, Brian de Bois-Guilbert. He thinks he loves her and that she should return the favor, but she resolutely refuses his seductive attentions.

As a result of a series of twisted circumstances, the evil Grand Master of the Templar Knights accuses her of being a sorceress. She's condemned and sentenced to die, to burn at the stake. Fate twists again: Her selfish kidnapper, Brian de Bois-Guilbert, who loved her but was scorned by her, now under orders from the evil Grand Master, himself has become, despite his own desires, her accuser. She will die unless a champion comes to save her.

The trumpets flourish. The herald cries. No champion appears for the beautiful Rebecca. She's offered one last chance to simply admit her guilt and be set free. She refuses. After all, the accusations aren't true. A delay is granted for one hour, and everyone waits with bated breath for the woman's fate.

Just as the hour is up and the stake is ready to burn, at the last moment, a rider, suited up in knight's armor, appears on a horse obviously worn out from hard riding. This would-be champion is so weak and weary he can hardly support himself in the saddle. Stopping in front of the Grand Master, the mystery man says, "I am a good knight and noble, come hither to sustain with lance and sword the just and lawful quarrel of this damsel, Rebecca . . . and to defy Sir Brian de Bois-Guilbert, as a traitor, murderer, and liar; as I will prove in this field with my body against his!"[5] The crowd catches their breath as the knight pushes back his helmet. It's Ivanhoe, barely healed. The Grand Master, an evil smile on his face, holds in his hand the gage of battle, the doomed maiden's glove; he throws it down with the fatal signal words, "Laissez aller!"

The knights charge at each other, lances held straight out for aim. Ivanhoe and his horse are just too weary for battle. The well-aimed lance of the Templar Knight strikes a blow, and Ivanhoe goes down. Rebecca covers her eyes and weeps. But to everyone's astonishment, Bois-Guilbert also reels in his saddle, loses his stirrups, and falls to the ground. Untouched, he dies, a judgment of God. The maiden is pronounced free and guiltless. She did have a champion, after all.

This story, shows Mains, parallels the dramatic biblical portrayal of the love story of a God and a people, the Divine Romance that begins with the Divine Deliverer who rescues his loved one at the last minute from the clutches of another evil Grand Master, the Pharaoh. A Champion appears, after all, and He frees her, this one called Israel who's bruised, chaffed, frightened, brutalized by bondage.

And when He saves her from certain death, do you know what He says to her? Leviticus 26:13: "I am the LORD your God, who brought you out of Egypt so that you would no longer be slaves to the Egyptians; I broke the bars of your yoke and enabled you to walk with heads held high."

As the drama unfolds, this mighty deliverance turns into a holy courtship as the Divine Deliverer begins to define a betrothal/engagement agreement. Imagine this, points out Mains. He, the great Lord, a most commanding potentate, is proposing marriage to the former slave girl of lowly nomadic origin. If she'll agree to set herself aside for Him; if she'll refuse to keep company with other men, not to look for other lovers; if she'll learn to love Him with her whole heart, soul, and strength; if she'll pledge herself to live a life different from all the other slave girls of common heritage, then He will covenant to be her husband, to betroth her to Himself, to bless her with His own personal riches, to endow her with His royal inheritance, to marry her at a future date, to celebrate the wedding feast at a special gathering of the nations of the world, and to keep the marital love warm, living, eternally lasting. What a story!

You see, the Old Testament is the story of the Divine Romance. The One Great Lord chooses a pitiful young woman because He sees her potential beauty, because He committed Himself to her family years before; He falls in love with her, draws her in merciful compassion into His arms, wipes the tears from her cheeks and speaks her special name, whispering that He has chosen her for His bride. There's nothing He would rather have than for her to follow Him the rest of her days.

Then what does He do? He gives her something very special to remind her of this betrothal/engagement covenant, a sign to her and to all the other lords that she's engaged to the One Great Lord, that she's taken. What is that special something?

Look what He says to her in Exodus 31:13: "This will be a sign between me and you for the generations to come, so you may know that I am the LORD, who makes you holy."

Chapter 8

Getting Engaged
to God

The word for sanctify in Exodus 31:13 is the same one used in Hebrew to describe marriage. Rabbi Heschel writes, "The Hebrew word *le-kadesh,* to sanctify, means, in the language of the Talmud, to consecrate a woman, to betroth."[1]

The implications of this are astounding! What God, the Divine Lover, is saying in this text is that the symbol He gives to His betrothed for her to put on as a reminder to her and to the world of their commitment to marriage, like an engagement ring, is the Sabbath. Putting the word *marriage* in the text, it now says "Observe my Sabbaths. This will be a sign between me and you for the generations to come, so you may know that I am the LORD, who sets you apart to marry you!"

This introduces a fresh, new approach to understanding the Sabbath and its role in God's covenant with His people. It places the Sabbath in the context of the Divine Romance between God and His people. Without this perspective, Sabbath keeping too easily degenerates into a legalistic obligation and duty. Any possible prohibitions concerning Sabbath activities will be seen in a purely negative light.

Richard Davidson also alludes to this picture of the Sabbath as a vital element in our love relationship with God. Commenting on the text in Isaiah 58:13, which refers to the Sabbath as a day of "delight," he portrays this perspective: "The word oneg ('delight') means literally 'exquisite delight,' and in its only other OT occurrence as a noun describes the palaces of royalty. In truth, on Sabbath we have an appointment with the King of kings!"

Then Davidson goes on to describe the King coming to honor us with His presence for a whole day each week, inviting us to His palace for an all-day spiritual feast and fellowship. Adding the final brush stroke to this glorious picture, he has this royal Personage choosing us as His lover, to be His bride. God invites us for intimate fellowship—an all-day date with the King.[2]

Earlier in his book, Davidson says that because God longs to celebrate with us a love relationship more intimate than anything human lovers have ever experienced, because He loves us so much that He can't wait a whole year or even a month for special time with us, "so every week He has set aside a whole day, a Sabbath, for intimate fellowship—an all-day date with us, His beloved."[3]

In researching the ancient Jewish marriage customs, especially the aspect of betrothal and engagement, Karen Mains discovered some significant implications:

> When discussing the idea of sanctification as holy betrothal, of God to a people or to us as individuals, it is important to understand ancient Jewish marriage customs as contrasted to our culture in which a young woman is engaged on an average as often as three times. According to what Alfred Edersheim writes in *Sketches of Jewish Social Life in the Days of Christ,* "From the moment of her betrothal, a woman was treated as if she were actually married. The union could not be dissolved, except by regular divorce; a breach of faithful-

ness was regarded as adultery; and the property of the woman became virtually that of her betrothed, unless he had expressly renounced it." He points out that the Mishnah (early written Jewish authority) describes regular writings of betrothal which stipulated the mutual obligations, the dowry, and all other points on which the parties had agreed. The author feels that it is safe to conclude that these New Testament betrothal customs were derivative from OT customs and similar in their formality. The betrothal in ancient Jewish culture, therefore, was a legally formalized, seriously bonding premarital pact.[4]

The application of these findings is especially significant. Being sanctified before the Lord, or being holy as unto Him or being set apart for Him, is hard for many of us to understand as a purely theological concept. But if we say our relationship to him is as though we're married to Him, and keeping the Sabbath is a sign of this, a celebration that we enact so we'll not forget, so we'll be reminded of this holy union—then suddenly, being sanctified takes on a whole new mental image that's perhaps easier to understand.

Because marriage is a common human symbol, most people understand, at least vaguely, what it means to be married. Husbands and wives know what it means to give themselves to another, to not desire any other, to live their lives around another, to put the good of that person before their own good.

Karen Mains comments:

Observing the Sabbath is like wearing an engagement ring. This ring we wear in weekly celebration not only reminds us that we're married to another (or betrothed with the same seriousness as in a marital covenant); it's not only a symbolic seal that binds us to our vows of spiritual fidelity, but Sabbath-keeping is the ring we put on that protects us from the seducing attentions of this evil world.[5]

Why does God deliberately choose the word *sanctify* with its marriage overtones to describe how the Sabbath fits into His relationship with us? Isn't it to place the context of His love for us in marriage terms to help us understand the power and passion of His love for us? Isn't it to help us appreciate His desire for our love and to help us see what a tremendous gift the Sabbath can be in helping us remember that incredible relationship?

Rabbi Heschel writes, as noted in the previous chapter, that the idea of the Sabbath as a queen or a bride is not a personification of the Sabbath but an exemplification of a divine attribute, an illustration of God's need for human love: "It does not represent a substance but the presence of God, His relationship to man."[6] The Sabbath is a continual reminder that God needs us, and we need Him.

All love stories, whether ancient or modern, whether fiction or true, are but pale imitations and impoverished comparisons to this cosmic drama, this Divine Romance between God and His people. Notice how at the heart of God's messages to His people through the prophets is the experience of marriage to illustrate His appeals:

"Your Maker is your husband. . . . For the LORD has called you like a wife forsaken and grieved in spirit, like a wife of youth when she is cast off " (Isaiah 54:5, 6, RSV).

Throughout the book of Isaiah the persistent, purposeful love of God holds out the promise that His desolate people will receive a new name, *Beulah*, Hebrew for "married"; and her God will rejoice over her as the bridegroom rejoices over the bride (62:4, 5).

The book of Jeremiah stresses the awful desolation of the land, which was imminent for Judah and Jerusalem by contrasting it with the joy and merriment of the wedding feast—the "voice of mirth and the voice of gladness, the voice of the bridegroom and the voice of the bride" shall cease (Jer. 7:34, RSV; 16:9; 25:10). In another context a poet describes the "garments of salvation" as bridal attire (Isa. 61:10).

The use of the figure of marriage to express the relationship between Yahweh and Israel is invaluable in articulating the divine love. Yahweh speaks to Israel through His prophet: "I remember the devotion of your youth, your love as a bride, how you followed me in the wilderness" (Jer. 2:2, RSV). Here the past is idealized by the prophet, and Israel is depicted as the devoted, faithful bride of her Lord and Redeemer.

This use of the husband concept to emphasize the relational theology of the covenant is brought out clearly in the book of Hosea. Here it is written that Yahweh the husband has repudiated his conjugal relation with his wife, Israel (Hos. 2:2), but that he will again betroth her to himself when she abandons her faithless practices (vss. 19-20). Then she will 'know the Lord' in a deeply personal and ethical way comparable to the knowledge which a man has of his wife.[7]

So beginning on the stage of the Old Testament and continuing with a "second act" performed on the platform of the New Testament is the story of the Divine Romance. Here, on the second stage, a tender young woman bears God's Son, a man child who takes on flesh to continue the wooing and courting in a way that can be seen. He, too, is the ultimate Gentleman Caller now in human form.

Ironically, when He grows up, He performs His first rites of divinity at a marriage feast, turning the water to wine for the wedding guests. Through His ministry, He continues to use the marriage experience to describe the nature of God's kingdom: the parable of the marriage feast (Matt. 22:1-14), the story of the wise and foolish maidens (Matt. 25:1-12).

And finally, He, too, becomes a Deliverer, a Champion, and proves Himself a victor in the battlefield of Calvary against the tempter, the traitorous seducer, the Grand Master of evil, Satan himself. Like Ivanhoe, He redeems His beloved, the world, at all cost, with His own body as forfeit.

The second act continues:

> In the NT use of marriage for theological definition of the gospel, Paul's words are significant: "I betrothed you to Christ to present you as a pure bride to her one husband" (2 Cor. 11:2). In admonishing his readers as to the proper relations between a husband and his wife, the writer of the Letter to the Ephesians states that "the husband is the head of the wife as Christ is the head of the church, his body" (Eph. 5:23). This affirms more than mere control, as vs. 25 shows—husbands are to love their wives, as Christ loved the church, and tenderly nourish and cherish them. With this background of the biblical use of marriage, the seer who has visions of the end time is able to announce that the marriage of the Lamb and his bride is about to be consummated; Christ and the faithful are to be united in marriage (Rev. 19:7-9). This union marks the appearance of the church triumphant, for the description of which the writer turns to the experience of marriage.[8]

To miss this motif of the Divine Romance etched into the drama of the Old and New Testaments is to miss God's whole love scheme—and it will result in being unprepared for the last and final act in the drama—the marriage celebration of the wedding of the bride and the Bridegroom.

To misunderstand this love scheme is to misunderstand the significant role of Sabbath. For Sabbath is the symbol a loving God, the Divine Romancer, gives His chosen one, the one He loves, to wear. It's a continual reminder to her, through the long days of waiting, of His betrothal agreement—a sign to her and to all the other eager young lords, the overly attentive suitors, that she's already engaged to, she's already set apart for, this One Great Lord. She belongs to Him—and everyone knows it! This is what the Sabbath says.

The famous conductor Reichel was taking his choir and orchestra through their final rehearsal of Handel's beautiful and inspiring "Messiah." When the soprano soloist came in with the refrain, "I know that my Redeemer liveth," she sang it with absolute flawless technique, perfect breathing, clear enunciation.

After she finished her part, everyone felt like clapping. They looked at the conductor expecting to see his responses of approval. With a motion from his baton for silence, he walked over to the soloist and said, almost sadly, "My daughter, you don't really know that your Redeemer lives, do you?"

The lady was taken aback, embarrassed, and somewhat confused. She answered, "Why, yes, sir, I think I do."

"Then sing it!" cried Reichel. "Tell it to me so that I'll know you've experienced the joy and power of it!"

Then he motioned for the orchestra to begin, and this time she sang with a passion that gave unmistakable evidence of her personal love for the risen Savior and Lord. All the people listening were so moved they wept. The old master, his eyes wet with tears, said to her, "You do know—this time you've told me."[9]

What about us? Are we so in love with the One who's so in love with us that it's obvious to everyone? Does our attitude toward the Sabbath reflect our passion for the Divine Lover to whom we're engaged? Can this world look at us and say, "Sure enough! They belong to Him! They're already taken and proud of it!" Can we say to God with pride and passion, not just on Sabbaths but every day, "Yes! we belong to You!"

Chapter 9

Keep Me True!

I'll never forget July 4, 1975. I woke up feeling a mixture of extreme excitement and anxiety. This was the day I'd been planning for, for some time. I didn't quite know what to expect, in spite of the fact that I had all the details completely planned out.

First thing on my agenda was the phone call. My fingers trembled a bit as I punched the numbers. I'd hit those numbers countless times before. I couldn't believe it—the phone was ringing on the other end of the line. And then I really couldn't believe it—he answered the phone.

I cleared my voice. "Dr. Gingrich?" "Yes," the voice on the other end replied. "Uh, this is Greg calling." I was trying my best to sound confident—to make a good impression. That was very important right now!

"Well, hi, Greg! How are you?"

"Just fine, sir, thank you! Uh-m-m, I know you're awfully busy trying to get ready to go on vacation, but there's something I wanted to ask you before you left."

"Oh, that's fine, Greg. What's that?"

My palms were sweating, and the phone kept slipping. I cleared my throat again. O for a drink of water!

"Well, sir, I was wondering . . . that is, would it be all right . . . I mean, I would really like to ask you if I could marry your daughter today. I mean, not marry her today, but ask her today if she would marry me. That is, if I could have your permission."

Silence on the other end of the line. Was he needing someone to resuscitate him?

After what seemed to me like eternity, he said, "Well Greg, Gwen and I have been expecting this for a while. And we would consider it a privilege to have you as our son-in-law."

Incredible! I couldn't believe it! He said Yes! "Oh, thank you, Dr. Gingrich! Thank you! I'll do my best to be a good husband for you, I mean, for her! Thank you, sir!"

Now I was really ready to begin! This was it! Part 2 of my plan. I got all my camera equipment together. After all, this momentous event had to be captured on film. I got the picnic basket with the Martinelli's sparkling cider and the two goblets—just in case she said Yes and we could celebrate. And most important of all, I picked up that little box and opened it just to make sure that beautiful watch was still there.

That watch. I remembered getting it only a month or so before this day. What an exciting day that was! I met my folks in Salem, Oregon—they lived in Portland, and I was an associate pastor down in Medford for the summer. They were so excited to be able to be involved with me in picking out the symbol of our engagement. We went through a number of jeweler's stores looking and searching. It took a lot of time because it had to be just right. And then finally I saw it—not the most expensive watch in the world; on my college student's budget not a whole lot was possible. But it was beautiful to me—gold-colored like Cindy's gold hair, a petite band like her petite waist, a cute crystal face just like her cute face, and the watch was a

Seiko at that! (I was born in Japan and was partial to Japanese watches!) What a feeling to put my hard-earned money down on the counter and then take that watch in the rose-colored box out of the store with me.

All those memories flooded my mind as, that July 4 morning, I hid the watch box in the trunk of the car. This was it! All systems go!

The car was ready, everything was packed, so calling Cindy, we finally were off. As fast as my little '68 VW beetle could go, I drove to the Oregon coast and then down to the quaint town of Crescent City, California. There's something about the coast that's very romantic to me.

As we pulled into the picturesque little town, my heart began thumping wildly. This was it! The moment I had been living for. I almost couldn't believe it was really happening. Cindy sat beside me still unsuspecting. I was afraid my pounding heart would give it away!

I drove up to the old lighthouse overlooking the ocean and the town. It was abandoned at the time. "Perfect!" I said to myself.

As we got out of the car, I was trying to figure out how in the world I could get that watch box in my coat pocket without her seeing. I gathered up all my camera equipment, and we started walking up to the lighthouse. The watch was still back in the trunk.

Halfway there, I stopped and said, "Oh, Cindy, I left something in the car. You go on, and I'll go get the stuff and be right back."

Opening the trunk, I tried to jam this box into my jacket pocket. It was really too big to fit. It bulged way out. "Oh well, I'll try to cover it with my arm."

We got situated on some rocks by the lighthouse—the view was incredible, looking out over the ocean, the surf breaking on the sand and rocks below, the sea gulls singing, every once-in-a-while the fog-horn blowing, the little town below just starting to come to life.

I thought to myself, "All right, Greg, this is it! No turning back now! Go for it, man! You can do it! Come on, you've been waiting and planning for this moment! Everything's just right! Now get down on your knees and go for it!"

Cindy was looking off into the distance, so I pulled and tugged on that crazy box stuck in my pocket. It finally came out. Handing it to Cindy, I said, "Here, Cindy, this is for you."

She had kind of a surprised and quizzical look on her face as she took the box. She opened it. Boy, did it look nice! The watch read, 12:05 p.m.

My heart was really beating now! I took her hands, sank to my knees next to the rock, and stammered, "Cindy, would you marry me?"

To this day, I still cannot remember what she said, I was so nervous. But she must have said Yes, because here we are married, with three children today! And I have pictures to prove it all. What a feeling!

The Martinelli's tasted better than ever! The lunch in town was fantastic. The trip back to Medford in my trusty '68 Beetle, late Friday afternoon, was wonderful—until, in the midst of our ecstasy, we heard a loud noise coming from the engine: bang, bang, bang, bang, bang!

I pulled off to the side of the road, got out of the car, and lifted the trunk to look inside at the engine, as though I knew a lot about engines and could figure out what was wrong by a quick look!

I didn't know anything, except that the engine was still there and it was making a terrible noise and I didn't think the car should be driven any farther. Something was definitely wrong, that was for sure. My heart sank! We were out in the middle of nowhere as far as I knew. I had just gotten engaged to the most wonderful girl in all the world. Now what should I do? Gathering our belongings together, we stood beside the road and stuck out our thumbs.

Cars continued to drive by without stopping. I couldn't figure it out—passing such a nice-looking couple stranded beside the road out in nowhere, a couple that had just gotten engaged besides? *How could this be,* I thought!

Finally an old man in a pickup stopped. He said he would take us to the nearest town. We got in. He asked us if we'd had a hard time getting a ride. That was putting it mildly, I thought. He said nobody around here stopped for hitchhikers because there was a Satanist commune in the area and there had been several murders recently.

"Oh great," I thought to myself, "This is good! I'm hitchhiking in a satanic area in the middle of nowhere with my brand new fiancée! Good work, Greg!"

He dropped us off at a phone booth in this tiny town. The sun was beginning to set on the greatest day of our lives. We were still so ecstatic, the full impact of our predicament hadn't really set in. Calling my senior pastor and informing him of our situation and whereabouts, he told me to hang tight, and he would come to pick us up. It would take several hours to get there.

So guess what we did while we waited? No, we didn't go searching for a repair garage to fix our car. As the fireworks were booming and blasting overhead, we crammed ourselves into the little phone booth and called everyone we could think of in the world—collect, of course—to tell them, WE'RE GETTING MARRIED, WE'RE GETTING MARRIED! We didn't even mention the car, strangely enough. Somehow, that didn't seem to matter. WE WERE GETTING MARRIED, and Cindy had the watch to prove it—that's all that mattered! July 4—Independence Day!

So was all this engagement ritual that day, and the days of preparation before, worth all this trouble? No question about it in our minds! That whole process, now symbolized by the watch Cindy was wearing on her wrist, was a regular reminder that we had pledged to each other loving commitment—that she was taken. I had taken her and she had accepted to become unavailable to anyone else.

We wanted no one else. Every time she looked at her watch, which was often, since we're all creatures of time and which she had to do deliberately since it was now on her right hand instead of on her left, she was reminded of our commitment to each other.

One of the greatest truths of Scripture is that God is a Divine

Lover wooing and courting His people. He wants a marriage commitment. He wants to exchange vows of exclusive love and loyalty. His passion for His mate burns within His heart.

Notice the incredible picture of this described in Hosea. 'In that day,' declares the LORD, 'you will call me "my husband"; you will no longer call me my master (2:16, NIV). He then goes on to describe the kind of relationship He wants with His people: " 'I will betroth you to myself for ever, betroth you in lawful wedlock with unfailing devotion and love; I will betroth you to myself to have and to hold, and you shall know the Lord' " (2:19, NEB).

What a picture of God's love for us—the engagement experience He wants with us. But the impact of this picture is even greater when we understand the ancient Jewish marriage customs. As we noted chapter 8, once a Jewish woman in Bible times was engaged, it was as though she were already married. Only a divorce could call off the wedding. If she were unfaithful, it was the same thing as unfaithfulness in marriage.

This concept helps us to understand, for example, why Joseph was so upset when he found out Mary was pregnant, and he knew he wasn't the father. In his mind (and he knew it would also be in the minds of the whole community), she had committed adultery, even though they were engaged and not yet married.

That's why he had to consider divorce to end their engagement. That was the law. A betrothal contract could only be dissolved through divorce or death. That's how seriously they took the engagement experience.

For this reason, throughout the Bible, unfaithfulness to God is described as spiritual adultery, breaking the betrothal/engagement vows of exclusive commitment and loyalty to each other.

The outward evidence

Because God takes this engagement commitment so seriously and wants us to be just as serious, He gives us something to help us remember. God gives to His beloved a symbol of His engagement, like the watch I gave to Cindy or the ring many others give each other. Why? So that His beloved will have a pledge of His enduring love and a reminder that she belongs to Him. That engagement symbol, that watch, that ring, is the Sabbath.

Notice Exodus 31:13, RSV—God says, "You shall keep my Sabbaths, for this is a sign between me and you throughout your generations, that you may know that I, the Lord, sanctify you."

As mentioned above, the Hebrew word for sanctification is the same as the word for marriage. In fact, Heschel said, "In the Friday evening service we say, 'Thou hast sanctified the seventh day,' referring to the marriage of the bride to the groom. Sanctification is the word for marriage."[1]

What God is saying in Exodus 31:13 is, "I am giving you the Sabbath as the sign that you and I are engaged to be married, that I am the One who sets you apart to be married to me."

The same thing is repeated in Ezekiel 20:12, 20—"Also I gave them my Sabbaths as a sign between us, so they would know that I the LORD made them holy. . . . Keep my Sabbaths holy, that they may be a sign between us. Then you will know that I am the LORD your God."

The spiritual implications are astounding! Like the watch Cindy wore or like the ring many wear, every time we come to the Sabbath, we're reminded of who we belong to—that we have been set aside by a passionate God to enjoy His love and blessings forever.

Like Cindy and I did, scrunched together in that little phone booth on July 4, shouting into the phone to whomever answered and would listen, "WE'RE GETTING MARRIED, WE'RE GETTING MARRIED," so every Sabbath we come together, our families unite, our souls are retuned to the great love song that sings out to the world, "WE'RE ENGAGED TO THE GREAT GOD OF THE UNIVERSE; WE'RE GETTING MARRIED; WE BELONG TO EACH OTHER; I AM HIS AND HE IS MINE; HIS BANNER OVER ME IS LOVE!"

So imagine the pathos, now, in the story of Hosea as he watches his betrothed, his beloved, leave him and begin running around with other lovers. Chapter 2 describes this affair. Hosea's heart aches as he sees her acting as though all the good things she's enjoying are from those lovers, when in fact they're from him.

And as if that weren't bad enough, he sees her take the silver and gold he has given her as gifts and symbols of their engagement and sees her give them to her lovers.

In other words, she takes her engagement watch or ring and gives it to another man. Can you imagine how painful that must be?

This whole story is a picture of God's passion and longing for His beloved and His heartache from her unfaithfulness. So, you see, to neglect the Sabbath, to take it lightly, to trample on it, is like Cindy taking that watch and refusing to wear it or laughing at it every time she looks at it or throwing it on the ground and stomping on it or giving it to another man as a token of her love for him.

On the contrary, in our situation, Cindy wore that July 4 watch proudly, refusing to take it off for fourteen years, even when it began keeping lousy time. She kept taking it in to get fixed because she didn't want to replace it.

Actually, it finally got so expensive to keep fixing we decided a couple of years ago she should buy a new one. But she still has that engagement watch in a special place, and it still conveys to her a special significance.

This is why God places such value on the Sabbath. It's not some kind of legalistic obligation, some kind of meaningless duty we have to perform because the fourth commandment tells us to. It's a gracious gift, a perpetual reminder, a hedge of protection against unfaithfulness, from the Divine Romancer, the One who has committed Himself exclusively to His loved one. It's a gift from the One who has promised to carry this engagement/betrothal experience all the way to its joyous consummation at the great Wedding Feast between the Bride and the groom when Jesus comes again.

Only those who have committed themselves to God and have accepted His covenant of love can really keep the Sabbath, because only those people will wear the Sabbath watch or ring with pride and devotion. Only when we see the gospel at the heart of the Sabbath will the Sabbath make sense, will we see it for what it really is. Maybe for some of us, this is the very first time.

Arturo Toscanini was once the most famous orchestra conductor in the United States. In 1931, during the days of radio, NBC invited Toscanini to conduct a concert tour of Latin America.

The day came for the musicians, gathered from orchestras across the country, to begin rehearsing Beethoven's renowned Sixth Symphony. These were professional musicians who knew the music like the back of their hands. They knew where to come in and where to rest. They knew where they could get up and take a walk and still be back in time to come in at their part.

But when Toscanini began to direct, something happened. By the end of the first movement, everybody could sense it. No one was daydreaming; all of them were intent on the music. They played as if it were entirely new. They came to the final movement and the grand finale, and when the maestro laid down his baton, the members of the orchestra were so moved they rose spontaneously to their feet and broke into thunderous applause. "Bravo! Bravo!"

Toscanini stood there until the applause stopped. Then he said to the orchestra, "That's not Toscanini, that's Beethoven. You just never heard him before."[2]

When we begin to see the Sabbath in the way God meant for us to, as a love day, a day to adore the One who is so in love with us, a gift from the One with whom we are engaged to be married, it's as though we're seeing the Sabbath for the first time. It's always been there, we just never really saw it like this before! This is the First Love experience. Through a continual "remembering" of the Sabbath, it can be kept alive!

This is what God's people should really want, to "wear" this symbol with pride, shouting out to the world, "We're already taken, we're engaged, we're going to be married, to be set apart for, saved for, sanctified to Another! We are not our own. We belong to God! 'To You only, God, will we cling—now and forever!' "

The inward attitude

In Elie Wiesel's novel, *The Town Beyond the Wall,* a Jewish mother and her young son were trying to escape the Nazis, so they decided to hide themselves in a farm wagon covered with hay to get across the border.

Before getting into the wagon, the mother took her son's head between her hands, looked him solemnly in the eyes, and warned him, "We must be silent, son. Whatever happens! It's our only chance. Our lives depend on it! Even if you're afraid, even if you're hurt, don't call out and don't cry! Do you understand?"

The little five-year-old boy, trying to be as brave as possible, nodded his head Yes. The mother and son climbed into the wagon, and the farmer covered them up with a huge pile of hay. Their bumpy journey toward freedom began.

Suddenly the wagon stopped. The mother and son held their breaths, knowing they had come to the border. The guards walked around the wagon, eyeing the farmer and his load suspiciously. Finally, after what seemed like an eternity, one of the guards, noticing the nervousness of the driver, asked what else he was carrying.

"Nothing at all," he said. The guards weren't convinced. Drawing their swords, they began plunging them indiscriminately into the hay until the farmer winced in fear. Seeing this, the guards started throwing the hay off the wagon, emptying it. There was the little boy, tears streaming down his face, still sitting quietly in a pool of his own blood.

He cried out, "Mamma, it wasn't me who called out! It wasn't me, Mamma!" But his mother did not reply. She had already died from the stabs.[3]

Both had been silent for the sake of the other in spite of the pain. That's the power of love—a commitment to be faithful no matter what the cost, no matter how hard it might be.

This is the kind of loyalty and commitment that God, the Divine Romancer, longs for us to have with Him—an exclusive attachment that refuses to be unfaithful regardless of the costs.

Brennan Manning challenges us with this illustration:

Suppose it were so ordained that your whole future, your eternal destiny was to depend on your personal relationship with the bishop of your area [or we could also say, for illustration's sake, one of your teachers, or a friend, or employer—in other words, everything to do with your eternity hinged on your relationship with this one special person]. Wouldn't you arrange to spend considerably more time with him than you do now? Wouldn't you try with his help to overcome all the character defects and personality traits that you knew were displeasing to him? And suppose business obligations [or some kind of assignment] called you away to . . . [the far away city of] New York, wouldn't you drop him frequent notes from there, and be eager to return to him?

And if he confided to you that he kept a diary of personal memoirs, which were the deepest whisperings of his inner self, wouldn't you be anxious not only to read them but to steep yourself in them so that you might know and love him more?

These are burning questions that every disciple must answer in total candor. Do you hunger for Jesus Christ? Do you yearn to spend time alone with Him in prayer? Is He the most important person in your life? Does He fill your soul like a song of joy? Is He on your lips as a shout of praise? Do you eagerly turn to His memoirs, His personal testament, His Gospels to learn more of Him? Are you making the effort to die to anything and everything that would inhibit, diminish, or threaten your friendship?[4]

Those are difficult questions to answer, aren't they? Perhaps they're difficult to respond to because they call into focus the central issue in all of our relationships—that of faithfulness and commitment.

Back in 1970, our family, living in Asia as missionaries, returned to the United States for a three-month furlough. I'd just finished my sophomore year in high school and would be returning to Far Eastern Academy in Singapore at the end of the summer for my junior year. Halfway through that sophomore year I'd started dating a girl, and I guess you could say that by the end of the year we were basically going steady (whatever that means).

Toward the beginning of our furlough, our family went to Atlantic City for the quinquennial General Conference Session of the Seventh-day Adventist Church. There are several things I particularly remember about that session, none of them involving the meetings in the auditorium, however.

I remember working for one of the display booths as a salesman. I had never done that before and kind of enjoyed it. I remember running around the Boardwalk at nights, looking in the shops, going to the amusement park, and just basically having a lot of fun.

But what stands out in my mind the most was meeting this really cute girl whose sister my older brother had started dating while there. Their parents were attending the General Conference Session too. It was kind of convenient, my brother and I seeing two sisters. I couldn't believe how cute she was!

We started spending some time together, but the whole time we were together, I felt terribly guilty because I was still going steady with my girlfriend from academy.

One night, the four of us were sitting in a small pizza parlor on the Boardwalk when my worst nightmare came true. I'd been worrying about this the whole time I'd started seeing this girl. Some people from Singapore whom I knew and who knew my academy girlfriend and knew we were dating walked into the restaurant.

I could not believe it! I tried to turn my face away, hoping they wouldn't recognize me. But to my chagrin, they walked over to our table and said Hi! And then to make matters worse, they started asking me if I'd heard anything from my girlfriend. My head was spinning, my hands were sweating, my heart was coding. No way out this time! My life was over!

Well, as it turned out, I survived that episode; although, unfortunately, I didn't see that girl again. When I got back to school in the fall, my girlfriend had heard about me, and we spent a lot of time talking about it. But I'll never forget those feelings at Atlantic City— I felt so guilty, so unfaithful!

Oh, the joys and pains of young love! But how important the issue of faithfulness and commitment is, especially when it comes to earthly marriage and to our spiritual marriage.

It's not easy maintaining exclusive loyalty and commitment, in action as well as thought, in a world that thrives on infidelity. Look at the literature of the world, notice the television media. Researchers tell us that 80 percent of all sexual acts implied or portrayed on TV are outside the context of marriage. On TV or in the movies, if two people go out with each other and feel an attraction at all, it's just assumed they're going to end up in bed together. Simple as that!

An hour or two of listening to much of today's popular music reveals the mournful wailing over broken vows, philandering women and womanizing men, songs that summarize in down-to-earth terms the mourner's dirge over the grave site of a once-promised faithful love.

The world thrives on infidelity, unfaithfulness. No wonder it's so hard to maintain vows of exclusive commitment in action and in thought.

Orthodox Jews have a strategy to try to deal with that. Almost obsessively, they remind themselves of God's fidelity agreement with them by tying little boxes containing scripture on their head and arms every weekday morning, during morning prayers. They do this because of the various commands from the Old Testament such as "bind [my words] as a sign upon your hand, and they shall be as frontlets between your eyes" (Deut. 6:8, RSV). So they use leather cords to wrap these little boxes around their heads, forearms, and hands. Phylacteries, they're called.

We may smile at this kind of literalism. But every day, as the Jew puts these on himself and wraps his prayer shawl tightly around him, he prays, "Hear O Israel, the Lord your God, the Lord is One. And you shall love the Lord your God with all your heart, and with all your soul, and with all your might."

As he continues winding the strap around himself, he repeats God's words from Hosea, "And I will betroth you to me for ever . . . and you shall know the Lord." (2:19, 20, RSV). Rituals performed every day.

Too literalistic? Too ritualistic? Perhaps. But the question is, what ways do we have to help remind ourselves of our vows of exclusive commitment and love to God? The above sections have shown how God's gracious gift of the Sabbath functions as that reminder of His great passion for us and our commitment of faithfulness to Him—the sign that we belong to each other.

The question is, how can our attitude toward the Sabbath, our experience of it, facilitate faithfulness and loyalty to Him regardless of circumstances or cost?

God had this plan from the very beginning. The first word in the fourth commandment is crucial in helping us maintain this commitment with our Divine Lover. What is that word? "Remember . . . Remember the Sabbath day to keep it holy."

Remember! Every time we remember the Sabbath, what should we be reminded of? As has been noted, we're reminded of God's exclusive vows of love and commitment to us—that He loves us no matter what, He loves us as we are, not as we should be. This is what Creation and redemption, the two events memorialized by the Sabbath, say to us. We're engaged to the great Lord of the universe. We belong to Him because He has chosen us! He's passionately in love with us! And we like it!

Paul Stevens, in his book *Marriage Spirituality: Ten Disciplines for Couples Who Love God*, makes a powerful parallel between our earthly marriage experience and the Sabbath. Referring to Dolores Leckey's suggestion that the physical union between husband and wife is the ritual of the marriage covenant,[5] he says "a marriage consummated only once on the wedding night and never again will not survive. The ritual of the covenant needs to be repeated again and again, just like Sabbath. We have short memories and need these powerful reminders."[6] Powerful reminders. Sabbath. Interesting concept!

That must be why God says, "Remember the Sabbath day." The Sabbath is graciously given to us as that powerful reminder of our covenant vows of love and commitment to God. So how does that work?

Karen Burton Mains, in her book on making Sabbath special, stresses that if the Sabbath is the high point of the week, as the biblical example shows it to be, then we should spend three days getting ready (called preparing for the bride) and three days afterward remembering it (called the delight of the wedding). She diagrams this "rhythm of the sacred" in this way:[7]

ANTICIPATION	CELEBRATION	REFLECTION
The "Observe" of		The "Remember of
Deuteronomy 5:12:		Exodus 20:8:
Wednesday, Thursday, Friday	Sabbath	Sunday, Monday, Tuesday

So the rhythm of the sacred is ANTICIPATION—CELEBRATION—REFLECTION. What are the implications?

She explains that the more persistently we practice the discipline of preparing for the Sabbath in the three days preceding it and the more thoroughly we enjoy its benefits in the three days following it, the more delightfully restful the Sabbath itself will be for us in its actual practice. And not only the Sabbath becomes transformed. Our faithful anticipation and remembrance of the Sabbath end up transforming the entire week.

ANTICIPATION—CELEBRATION—REFLECTION. Richard Davidson has captured the essence of this experience, as well, when he writes:

> The mood is one of expectancy. The Shabbat is the day around which all the other days of the week revolve. We feel ourselves sheltered in the shadow of the past Shabbat until Tuesday, and from Wednesday on the family already basks in the light of the approaching Shabbat.[8]

ANTICIPATION—CELEBRATION—REFLECTION. In other words, the Sabbath experience and all it stands for, as it is remembered and reflected upon throughout the week, has the potential of transforming all of life. "The Sabbath is the inspirer, the other days the inspired."[9] And correspondingly, referring to that potential, Ellen White writes, "We are not merely to observe the Sabbath as a legal matter. We are to understand its spiritual bearing upon all the transactions of life."[10]

By remembering and cultivating the presence of Christ in all activities (whether these be worshipping, talking, eating, walking, reading, listening to music, visiting, etc.), the believer experiences and celebrates the holiness of the Sabbath; that is, "the manifestation of God's personal presence in his life. The consciousness of the nearness of God quickens and brings into life all that is purest and best."[11]

Karen Burton Mains reinforces this aspect of the Sabbath and its impact on all of life when she says that by observing the Sabbath in this way we make prayer through the rest of the week more possible; it marks one day as being holier than the others, enabling us, consequently, to sanctify the other moments of weekly time. "Here in this sanctuary in time, we are reminded that the spiritual other world in reality exists. Prepared for it, we can step into it."[12]

So Sabbath ANTICIPATION—CELEBRATION—REFLECTION is a powerful tool, a gift from God to help us faithfully remember Him, to prepare for His presence.

The Duchess of Windsor had a very unique style of hospitality. This compulsively organized woman left nothing to chance. Invitations issued by telephone were followed by an engraved card that read: "This is to remind you that the Duke and Duchess of Windsor expect you on such and such a date, for the weekend at teatime."

The guesthouse had two bedrooms and two baths. A female guest was housed in the pink room supplied with pink soap made especially for the Duchess, along with bath salts, medicinal supplies, fresh flowers, and air freshener wrapped in a terry-cloth to match the towels.

A male guest was housed in the yellow bedroom decorated with walls of soft felt and matching draperies. His room contained a bar and his bathroom held all the necessary shaving tools with bottles of shaving lotion and cologne arranged with their tops already removed.

Guests were expected for tea, and then would return to the cottage to rest and dress before dinner. Once back in the cottage, a male guest would discover that his bags had been completely unpacked, his clothes freshly pressed, and his shoes polished. All the drawers and doors were open so that he could see at a glance where each item had been placed. His dress shirt would be laid out, studs in place, handkerchief folded, and in the dinner jacket breast pocket, socks turned inside out for the proper toe-first putting-on.

After a black-tie dinner, the guest would retire to his room where he would find a menu card on which he was asked to list what he wanted for breakfast and what time he wanted to be served. After filling out the card, it was to be placed outside the door to his room.

Breakfast was served in bed: in the pink and white bedroom, on white china with a pink strawberry motif, along with a small vase of pink and white flowers . . . and in the yellow bedroom, on yellow china with yellow flowers.[13]

Whatever the reactions might be to all of this detailed thought and preparation, at least it can be said that the Duchess of Windsor knew how to get ready for guests! It provides a pause for some serious thinking. She may have been obsessively compulsive about it all, and there may have been no warmth or love in it all, but think of it: all of that for earthly guests, maybe people she would never see again. Yet how much preparation do I do, in body and mind and atmosphere, for the King of the universe, my own God who so passionately loves me and is committed to me, who comes to my home as my special Guest every Sabbath, who comes to spend time with me, to talk with me, to enjoy my company? Is there ANTICIPATION—CELEBRATION—REFLECTION?

Could this be what God had in mind when He said, "Remember the Sabbath day to keep it holy?" It's as though He is saying, "Look, if you will just be deliberate and intentional in remembering the Sabbath and all it stands for, holiness in the rest of life will be no problem, because you'll be remembering Me, and I am the God who makes you holy!"

Maybe if we were as obsessed with our passion for God and our times with Him as the Duchess of Windsor was in preparing for her guests, we wouldn't have as much trouble with spiritual infidelity or unfaithfulness in our daily living.

So we can see that God has designed the Sabbath and our experience of ANTICIPATION—CELEBRATION—REFLECTION to be the safeguard against spiritual adultery. If we develop the ability to remember all through the week, through each day, learning intentionally to direct our thoughts to God and His continual presence, faithfulness to Him in both thought and deed will be a reality.

Marva Dawn writes:

> If I live each day longing for the special Sabbath day of celebrating his presence, I am much more aware throughout the week that he is with me. Ideally, all the attempts to be in control during the week are thwarted by the consciousness that each moment is leading toward the Sabbath and that each moment also derives its empowerment from the delight of the previous Sabbath. To live with such an attitude creates a lifestyle with an emphasis that is the opposite of the world's emphasis.[14]

The simple cook in the monastery, Brother Lawrence, was one who had developed this discipline of remembering. He learned to press spiritual meaning into virtually every action of his day. Note his capacity to see not only meaning but also purpose in even his menial activities:

> I turn my little omelet in the pan for the love of God. When it is finished, if I have nothing to do, I prostrate myself on the ground and worship my God, who gave me this grace to make it, after which I arise happier than a king. When I can do nothing else, it is enough to have picked up a straw for the love of God. People look for ways of learning how to love God. They hope to attain it by I know not how many different practices. They take much trouble to abide in His presence by varied means. Is it not a shorter and more direct way to do

everything for the love of God, to make use of all the tasks one's lot in life demands to show Him that love, and to maintain His presence within by the communion of our heart with His? There is nothing complicated about it. One has only to turn to it honestly and simply.[15]

"Remember the Sabbath day to keep it holy." God's safeguard for us against spiritual adultery and unfaithfulness to Him is in the process of remembering, living in the regular rhythm of the sacred, of ANTICIPATION—CELEBRATION—REFLECTION. It is work, though, isn't it? It takes effort and discipline.

For one thing, it takes the discipline of paying attention to God in the midst of the scores of worldly distractions. As Michael Warren notes, for a follower of Jesus, the discipline of spirituality in our time must in large part be the discipline not so much of praying effectively as of paying attention effectively to the proper matters. "Spirituality is a systematic way of attending to the presence of God."[16]

The discipline of remembering, mental fidelity to God, comes by intentional choices for focused attention, directed passion. A husband or wife, when separated from each other, must deliberately choose to be faithful to the other in both thought and behavior. How do they do it? They utilize every available symbol of their love and commitment to each other to help them remember (like a wedding ring, a watch, a picture, a favorite gift, a letter, a memory, a phone call).

Even so, we must choose to surround ourselves with spiritual symbols God graciously gives us, like the Sabbath, to help us faithfully remember, to help us sustain our love and commitment to Him. We must deliberately create around us "sabbathing" moments.

Gordon MacDonald emphasizes this experience when he suggests that Sabbaths can be short bursts of spiritual recollecting, reminding us of the quick pit stops of the Indianapolis racer when there is a need for fuel, tires, and refreshment. To "create the Sabbathing moment," even if it is a terribly brief one, is an all-important pursuit whether we're talking about mothers or business people or students.

"One thought in such a pause can be the big difference in how the next hours are going to be lived, whether they will be in spiritual passion or in drudgery."[17]

Deliberately creating the "Sabbathing moments" when the heart and mind are purposefully directed toward God and our love and commitment to Him is central to faithfully fulfilling God's command to "remember"—Sabbath ANTICIPATION—CELEBRATION—REFLECTION.

In writing to a friend in need of spiritual instruction, Francois Fenelon refers to the importance of this spiritual principle of intentionally creating the "Sabbathing moments" throughout the day, deliberately remembering God:

> You must learn . . . to make good use of chance moments, when waiting for someone, when going from place to place, or when in society where to be a good listener is all that is required; . . . at such times it is easy to lift the heart to God, and thereby gain fresh strength for further duties. The less time one has, the more carefully it should be managed. If you wait for free, convenient seasons in which to fulfill real duties, you run the risk of waiting forever; especially in such a life as yours. No, make use of chance moments.[18]

Mental fidelity has never been easy. It doesn't come naturally to the sinful, human spirit. So God graciously provides help: Sabbath ANTICIPATION—CELEBRATION—REFLECTION—a gracious gift from God Himself to help us remain faithful and free for Him in thought and action. Far from a legalistic obligation required by God, the Sabbath is a gift of grace from the Divine Lover who's so passionately in love with us and longs for us to feel the same about Him.

Dietrich Bonhoeffer wrote, "It is not your love that sustains the marriage; but from now on, the marriage that sustains your love."[19] Even so, God gives us a symbol of our mutual commitment, the Sabbath, which will serve as a tool to help sustain our spiritual relationship. "Remember the Sabbath day to keep it holy. . . ."

When God sets apart certain things as holy, He does it in such a way that it has the potential of imbuing with holiness and consecration every phase of life taking place beyond its confines. In the same way, "the Seventh Day was set apart from the six working days only so that its Sabbath spirit might permeate all of weekday life."[20]

This is why God wants us to remember the Sabbath. In remembering the Sabbath, we remember Him, and our focused attention on Him "consecrates" every other moment as well.

Directed passion—focused attention—that's the key, isn't it?

The story is told of a Moslem who was dying of thirst in the middle of the desert. Finally he came upon a well. Dropping the bucket beside the well down into its depths, with the little strength he had left, he pulled it up. To his amazement, it was full of silver, silver coins. He emptied the bucket, then dumped it into the well again. Pulling it up the second time, he couldn't believe his eyes. It was full of gold, sparkling, shining, rich.

This time the Moslem protested: "My Lord God, I know how powerful You are and what marvels You're capable of. But all I want is a cup of water!"

He emptied the bucket of gold, lowered it into the well the third time, and retrieved it again. It was full of water. He drank and quenched his thirst.

Now that's focused attention, directed passion! That's what it means to be laid waste, devastated by one desire, consumed by singleness of purpose. Purity of heart, says Soren Kierkegaard, is to will one thing—nothing else matters, not even the cost.

The Good News of the gospel, the story of the Divine Romance, is that this is the kind of passion God has for us. In spite of the fact that He has the whole universe to run, there's absolutely nothing that He allows to distract Him, even for a second, from showing His love and desire for us . . . nothing in all of heaven or earth, says the apostle Paul (Romans 8:35-39). That is indeed Good News!

We, too, need this kind of consuming passion for God, a one-track mind that refuses the seductions of the scores of worldly lovers vying daily for our attention and love. What would Christ say if He were asked (if anyone cared to ask Him) about modern Christendom's Sabbath worship? I think He would say: "Though we have a relationship, the church is no longer good at making love, and now even on Sabbath, My love day, I know she's thinking about other suitors." When Sabbath ceases to be a sign, when the day is really like any other day, although like a dutiful wife we go through the forms of love, it's as though we've taken off our wedding band and hidden it in the kitchen drawer.

I love the way Karen Mains puts it:

> We are in danger of becoming the wife who is no longer even dutiful in her love-making, the woman who all the other women on the block know is carrying on an illicit affair, sneaking off to motels in the afternoon. We are like this woman—another love has taken precedence in our lives.[21]

What a tragic picture of spiritual unfaithfulness, spiritual drought, where the fountain of passion has run dry! But thank God He has graciously given us the opportunity, through the Sabbath, to deliberately and intentionally remember and experience

Him not only once a week but at moments throughout every day. The flames of passion can be rekindled through regular Sabbath times in which we reaffirm to Him, in which our whole lifestyle shouts out, "We belong to You, Lord! You're in love with us . . . and we like it!"

Chapter 10

Playing Heaven
With God

With this concept of the Sabbath in mind, the questions now are, what does the true Sabbath keeper look like? What kind of a lifestyle will the Sabbath keeper have? With people who are so in love with the God of the Sabbath, who recognize and accept God's deep passion for them, what will be important to them, what values will they hold dear, what will be their emphasis in life? How can the Sabbath and a renewal of its observance impact the life of the church and its renewal?

Do you remember playing house when you were a child? It seems as if most children, at some point or another, engage in that age-old game. It's almost synonymous with childhood.

I remember playing house when I was growing up. One time in particular stands out in my memory. I was in second or third grade. We were living in a little farming village on the west coast of Japan. My dad was trying to plant a church in the nearby city of Toyama. We were the only Americans or foreigners around, so we always looked forward to when our special friends, the Vendens, would come to visit us. They had three children the same ages as the three of us Nelson kids. Perfect fun!

During one of their visits, my father was holding a stop-smoking clinic in town. So that evening, we all jumped into the car, the five of them and the five of us, and went to the meeting. All I remember about that meeting was the film that was shown. And all I remember about the film was one scene: this man, who'd been sick or had surgery, came home from the hospital, walked into the front door of his apartment building, and there at the top of the long stairway was his beautiful wife waiting for him. The music crescendoed to its climax as the man rushed up the stairs and the two of them embraced. Wow! What a scene! It impressed this third-grader, that's for sure!

So the next day, when several of us kids were playing inside, we, of course, wanted to play house, and guess what scene we had to imitate? I remember standing at the bottom of our long stairway, carrying my dad's briefcase, looking up at my favorite Venden girl standing at the top, trying her best to look ecstatic at my arrival "home." And then, dragging the briefcase, I went stumbling up the stairs clear to the top so we could have our as-grown-up-as-possible-but-awkward hug! Playing house. Ahh, what fun!

What is it about playing house that children enjoy so much? Perhaps it's that playing house puts them in the world of adults. While they're playing house, they're pretending, imitating the adult world. It's a way for them to experiment with what it might be like being Mom and Dad. After all, being grown-up is paradise, right?

So by playing house, children can transcend the present for a while to see what it might be like living in the future. For a few moments at least, they bring the future right into the present.

In the same way, says Paul Stevens in his book *Marriage Spirituality*, "just as children imitate their parents and 'play house,' believers imitate their heavenly Father by 'playing heaven' on the Sabbath."[1] This is an incredible concept! Playing heaven. Could this be what Sabbath keeping is all about—imitating our heavenly Father by "playing heaven?"

Interestingly, the Jews have, through the centuries, maintained this very concept from Scripture. Much of their religious literature portrays the Sabbath as being a foretaste of heaven.

Theodore Friedman, a former managing editor of *Judaism* and now the rabbi of Congregation Beth El in New Jersey, writes that while it finds a variety of expressions in Talmudic literature, all of them, in the end, give voice to the idea that the Sabbath is "the anticipation, the foretaste, the paradigm of life in the world-to-come. The very abundance of such statements is the surest evidence of how deep-rooted and widespread that notion was in the early Rabbinic period."[2]

Again, at the end of the Mishnah Tamid it says, "A Psalm, a song for the Sabbath-day—a song for the time-to-come, for the day that is all Sabbath rest in the eternal life."[3] Another early tradition states, "The seventh day is an indication of the world-to-come that is all Sabbath."[4]

In other words, the Sabbath is a present experience of the future heaven. This is further illustrated clearly in one of the ancient traditions in which Israel says to God, "Master of the World, if we observe the commandments, what reward will we have?' He says to them: 'The world-to-come.' They said to Him: 'Show us its likeness.' He showed them the Sabbath."[5]

So it's evident that the Jews have long viewed the Sabbath as a regular experience of the kingdom-to-come. That's precisely the point of the author of the book of Hebrews when, in chapter 4, after discussing the weekly Sabbath rest, he concludes, in verses 9 and 11, by saying, "There remains, then, a Sabbath-rest for the people of God. . . . Let us therefore make every effort to enter that rest."

It would appear that what he's saying is that the reality of the eternal Sabbath rest in heaven can begin to be experienced now through our regular Sabbath rests. So "playing heaven" through Sabbath keeping allows the future to invade the present.

So, how does this happen? It happens by following this incredible principle of Sabbath keeping called "playing heaven." Notice the implication of developing such a concept of Sabbath keeping. Friedman concludes by saying, "The Sabbath is at once the climax of that primordial time and the paradigm of the future time. Therefore, man should so conduct himself on the Sabbath as if the future time were already at hand."[6] What Friedman then does in his article is develop that theme by looking at the biblical references describing the Messianic age according to the prophets. He summarizes the primary qualities of that future kingdom in the following ways:

One, the Messianic age will be a time of extraordinary material abundance for God's people.[7] Amos declares, " 'The days are coming,' declares the LORD, 'when the reaper will be overtaken by the plowman and the planter by the one treading grapes. New wine will drip from the mountains and flow from all the hills. I will bring back my exiled people Israel; they will rebuild the ruined cities and live in them. They will plant vineyards and drink their wine; they will make gardens and eat their fruit'" (Amos 9:13, 14). The prophet Joel asserts, " 'In that day the mountains will drip new wine, and the hills will flow with milk' " (Joel 3:18).

Descriptions like these can be found repeatedly in Isaiah (6; 7; 30:23), in Jeremiah (31:12), and in Ezekiel (34:13, 14). "In sum, in the prophetic Messianic vision, man's material needs will be available without labor and toil, as they were to Adam in the Garden of Eden."[8]

Two, the Messianic age will be characterized by unbroken harmony with all existence, with God, with nature, and with people.[9] The prophet Hosea describes it, " 'In that day I will make a covenant for them with the beasts of the field and the birds of the air and the creatures that move along the ground. Bow and sword and battle I will abolish from the land, so that all may lie down in safety' " (Hosea 2:18).

The picture that Isaiah paints of extraordinary longevity of life in the kingdom-to-come (Isaiah 65:20) implies that there will exist peace and harmony between people, without the existence of violence and murder, death by unnatural means. Isaiah goes on to describe it, " 'The wolf and the lamb will feed together, and the lion will eat straw like the ox, but dust will be the serpent's food. They will neither harm nor destroy on all my holy mountain,' says the LORD" (65:25).

Consider the fact that before his disobedience, Adam lived in unbroken harmony with all existence—with God, with Eve, with nature, and the beasts of the field. But with his sin, a profound split occurs, setting him off in tension and conflict with all of life, even with himself. So "the essential meaning of the Messianic time is the overcoming, the resolution of that split and the restoration of the primordial harmony which man once knew."[10]

And three, a final characterization of the Messianic age as Friedman describes it is that, as the prophets repeatedly assure, in the final time all human physical infirmities will vanish.[11] "Then will the eyes of the blind be opened and the ears of the deaf unstopped. Then will the lame leap like a deer, and the mute tongue shout for joy" (Isaiah 35:5, 6).

It's significant that Jesus, when He inaugurated His public ministry on the Sabbath in the Capernaum synagogue, identified His ministry as the fulfillment of the Messianic prophecy pointing to the ushering in of the Messianic age. He quoted the prophet Isaiah (61:1, 2) who said, " 'The Spirit of the Lord is on me, because he has anointed me to preach good news to the poor. He has sent me to proclaim freedom for the prisoners and recovery of sight for the blind, to release the oppressed, to proclaim the year of the Lord's favor' " (Luke 4:18, 19).

Then, rolling up the scroll He had just read from and giving it back to the attendant, He sat down. The eyes of everyone in the synagogue were fastened on Him, and He began by saying to them, " 'Today this scripture is fulfilled in your hearing' " (vs. 21).

Jesus' example here, along with the examples pointed out from the Old Testament prophets by Friedman, emphasize the truth that the Sabbath rest experience in the present is meant to be a realization of the future Sabbath rest in God's kingdom. Sabbath keeping involves bringing the blessings and qualities of heaven into the present, as far as is possible.

"Playing heaven" as the principle of Sabbath keeping can be defined as conducting ourselves on the Sabbath as if the future time were already here. Now think about that for a moment. Sabbath keeping, "playing heaven," means living as if heaven were already here—deliberately and intentionally living the quality of heaven's life now, as much as possible.

As Friedman shows, and as Jesus' own ministry demonstrated, the qualities of the heaven-to-come that we do our best to bring into the present involve the issues of peace and harmony between people and God and people and people, the enhancement of the quality of life and health, environmental concern, the building of relationships, the sharing of wealth and abundance with the less fortunate.

What's this saying? The most important implication, as far as I am concerned, is this: True Sabbath keeping is a lifestyle, a way of living, not merely a list of dos and don'ts for only one day out of the week.

M. L. Andreason wrote, "The Sabbath should be a demonstration of the gospel in operation. . . . This raises the Sabbath question from being merely the observance of a day to the living of a life."[12]

This is where we as Seventh-day Adventists, for example, have so often fallen short (and I'm sure we're not alone in this. Those who do their best to keep a Sabbath each week no doubt have struggled with this issue). We've tended to be so preoccupied with our list of dos and don'ts on the Sabbath day that we've isolated the Sabbath from the rest of the week. We've tended to see Sabbath keeping as exclusively revolving around such issues as swimming or no swimming, biking or no biking, playing catch and throwing Frisbees or not, going out to eat or not, going to a store or not, and you can add numerous others to this list.

While some of those issues may be important to some of us, this narrow approach to Sabbath keeping has caused us to miss out on the vast experiential meaning of Sabbath and how being a Sabbath keeper relates to all of life.

Abraham Heschel, wrote, "All days of the week must be spiritually consistent with the Day of Days. All our life should be a pilgrimage to the seventh day; the thought and appreciation of what this day may bring to us should be ever present in our minds."[13]

Ellen White writes, "We are not merely to observe the Sabbath as a legal matter. We are to understand its spiritual bearing upon all the transactions of life."[14]

True Sabbath keeping and spirituality have to do with how we live our lives all through the week, not just one day out of the week. Maurice Blondel has said, "'If you want to know what a person really believes, don't listen to what he says, but watch what he does.' [Because] only the practice of faith can verify the belief of faith."[15]

This is why Michael Warren is profoundly on target when he writes that spirituality is a way of walking, a particular way of being in the world. The reason people so often fail in their attempts at *spiritual renewal* is that "they never let the new program affect their life structure. Similar to dieting, if the program fails to change, not just the way we think but the way we act, then it has no affect."[16]

True Sabbath keeping is a way of living, not just a way of believing—changing life, not just belief. A man who had been recently converted to Jesus was approached by an unbelieving friend. "So you've been converted to Christ, huh?" the unbelieving friend said rather sarcastically.

"Yes," the new convert answered.

"Well then, you must know an awful lot about Christ, huh? Tell, me, what country was He born in?"

"I don't know," the convert replied.

"What was His age when He died?"

"I don't know."

"How many sermons did He preach?"

"I don't know."

"Well you sure don't know much for a man who claims to be converted to Christ."

The convert hung his head and said, "You're right. I'm ashamed at how little I know about Jesus. But this much I do know: Three years ago I was a drunkard. I was in debt. My family was falling to pieces; they dreaded the sight of me. But now I've given up drink. We're out of debt. Our home is happy. My kids can't wait until I come home every night. All this Christ has done for me. This much I do know of Him!"[17]

The point is, to know is to be transformed by what you know! True Sabbath keeping is so much more than merely things you do and do not do one day out of the week. True Sabbath keeping is a way of walking through life, a lifestyle, living heaven's style of life now throughout the week—"playing heaven" with the God of heaven.

No wonder God is so hard on the Israelites in the Old Testament. Their religious life, their spirituality, their Sabbath keeping, had degenerated into a list of dos and don'ts performed one day out of the week, on the Sabbath. Notice what God says to them in Isaiah 58. This is an incredible chapter on God's concept of real Sabbath keeping. Notice the issues God feels are important in our worship of Him. They will be developed in greater detail in the sections ahead as we discuss what it means to really keep the Sabbath, what it's like when God's people really "play heaven."

God is speaking through the prophet Isaiah:

(1) " 'Shout it aloud, do not hold back. Raise your voice like a trumpet. Declare to my people their rebellion and to the house of Jacob their sins. (2) For day after day they seek me out; they seem eager to know my ways, as if they were a nation that does what is right and has not forsaken the commands of its God.' "

(Look God! See how well we keep the Sabbath. We're law-abiding, commandment-keeping people!)

" 'They ask me for just decisions and seem eager for God to come near them. (3) "Why have we fasted," they say, "and you have not seen it? Why have we humbled ourselves, and you have not noticed?" ' "

What the people are saying is, "Look God, we're keeping the Sabbath faithfully, we're worshipping You on the right day, fasting and humbling ourselves! Why aren't you listening to us? Why aren't You blessing us?" So God goes on to give the answer:

" 'Yet on the day of your fasting, you do as you please and exploit all your workers. (4) Your fasting ends in quarreling and strife, and in striking each other with wicked fists. You cannot fast as you do today and expect your voice to be heard on high. (5) Is this the kind of fast I have chosen, only a day for a man to humble himself? Is it only for bowing one's head like a reed and for lying on sackcloth and ashes? Is that what you call a fast, a day acceptable to the LORD?' "

What was Sabbath keeping to these people? It was exclusively one day out of the week for the purpose of humbling themselves before God without any thought for their relationship with the rest of the world. There was no joy or celebration, only sackcloth and ashes. It was a ritual of solemnity and rugged religiosity. The atmosphere of heaven was far away!

A prominent Adventist church, some years back, revamped one of their Sabbath church services to be more informal. They called it Sonburst Celebration. The first Sabbath they did this, the place was packed. Everyone wanted to see what radical things were going to happen in a service using a name with the "C" word, Celebration (a word which for a while symbolized a very intense and controversial issue among some circles in Adventist worship).

Even before people started coming that first Sabbath, there was a small group of folks who positioned themselves outside the church doors to hand out some tracts. The tracts basically said that we are living in the time of the Day of Atonement and God's judgment. So this is a time for solemnity, not celebration.

That's what these Israelites believed, too, about their worship. There was no more joy or celebration. Sabbath keeping was exclusively fasting and worship on Sabbath and nothing more. It didn't impact the rest of their lives at all. But God certainly didn't agree with them on either count. Notice what He says next:

(6) " 'Is not this the kind of fasting I have chosen' " (in other words, so here's what God wants for Sabbath keeping—here's what it means to "play heaven," to live heaven's lifestyle now—here's what's important to God): "to loose the chains of injustice and untie the cords of the yoke, to set the oppressed free and break every yoke? (7) Is it not to share your food with the hungry and to provide the poor wanderer with shelter—when you see the naked, to clothe him, and not to turn away from your own flesh and blood?' "

True Sabbath keeping, then, is a lifestyle, deliberate attempts to bring the qualities of heaven to this earth now, "playing heaven," where we enjoy the opportunity to imitate our heavenly Father and the values important to Him. So what values does this passage say are important to Him? People, justice, peace, equality, feeding-clothing-housing the less fortunate, environment, family, relationships. Active concern about these issues, says God, and applying His values to them is true Sabbath keeping.

The problem with the Israelites, and it's often our problem, too, as Michael Warren points out, is that we tend to separate spirituality from the world in which we live. We pay attention to the things of God in such a way that our attention is drawn away from those pressing human issues. Our Sabbath worship revolves around whether we can throw a ball or Frisbee or not, whether water that goes above the knees constitutes swimming and is that OK or not. That's a false spirituality. Sabbath keeping that does not pay priority attention to the pressing human issues, says this chapter in Isaiah, is not real Sabbath keeping.

How do you react to this? Some of us aren't used to looking at it in this light. But as Samuele Bacchiocchi writes in his book *Sabbath, Divine Rest for Human Restlessness,* the purpose of the Sabbath rest "is not merely a temporary recovery from simply mental or physical fatigue" (what we Adventists jokingly call Lay Activities time), "but a reflection of the 'rest' of God Himself (Exod. 20:11), appointed to aid human beings in regaining the Divine Image."[18] So our Sabbath rest involves becoming involved with God in helping to restore His image to the rest of the world, nature, and people.

Sabbath keeping, "playing heaven," is a deliberate and intentional lifestyle of allowing the peace and gladness of heaven to become revolutionizing principles in the here and now, not just one day a week, but every day.

Brennan Manning was at the Atlanta airport with a two-hour layover. Looking down at his shoes, he noticed how dirty they were. So he decided he'd better get a shoeshine to look more presentable to the group he was going to speak to.

An elderly black man shined his shoes for the going rate of $1.50. With his shoes now clean and shiny, Manning handed him two dollars and said, "Now you get up in the chair, and I'll shine your shoes."

The man said, "Huh? What?"

"I won't charge you," Manning replied.

The old man stared at him suspiciously. "What for, then?"

"Because you're my brother," Manning said.

The man really looked confused now. Finally he said, "Well, when I ain't busy the boss leaves me some shoes to shine. But thank you anyway."

Manning saw tears in the man's eyes. He reached out and hugged him, and the man said softly, "No white man ever talked to me like that before."[19]

That is Sabbath keeping, "playing heaven," in its purest form—bringing the values of heaven into life now, imitating our heavenly Father. It means choosing to imitate the Father even if it might not make any visible difference, because it's just what He would do.

When Daniel Berrigan, a Catholic priest who's been a real peace activist through the years, lectured at Loyola University in New Orleans several years ago, someone in the audience asked him, "Dan, why do you keep knocking yourself out for the peace movement? You've paid your dues. You've lost your reputation in many dioceses as a sound theologian, you've spent five years in the slammer for pouring blood on draft files in Maryland, your friends have scattered, your honor is questioned, and your health has deteriorated. Can you see any real change in the posture of the American government or in the hearts of people because of what you've done?"

Berrigan paused, reflected for a full minute, and then replied, "I cannot not do what I'm doing. I do it, not necessarily for any changes it might accomplish, but because it's the right thing to do."[20]

What is it that gives God's people the courage to keep "playing heaven" in the face of often discouraging odds in a world going crazy? God's people keep "playing heaven," they keep trying to imitate their heavenly Father by working to instill His values here on earth, simply because it's the right thing to do, it's what He would do.

Isn't this why kids play house and pretend to be Mom and Dad? They don't do it because they think dressing up and imitating parents are going to revolutionize the world. They do it because they want to be like Mom and Dad. They're playing house! And it's fun, besides!

This is the kind of passion God's people need. The passion to be like Him! The passion to want their Sabbath keeping to really reflect heaven and their heavenly Father's values! The passion to "play heaven" more often!

Charles Scriven, president of Columbia Union College in Takoma Park, Maryland, says that since the Sabbath tells us blessedness and peace are waiting for the people of God in the kingdom-to-come, that justifies trying to make things better today—in our personal relationships, in community situations, and even in world affairs.[21] Our hope of heaven through the Sabbath gives us "a passion for what is possible" now.[22]

So let's look in greater detail to what it would be like for God's people to really "play heaven." How does this concept of Sabbath keeping play itself out in the life of the church? How can we bring the qualities of heaven into the present through our Sabbath keeping?

Chapter 11

Playing Heaven
With the Family

Among the written prayer requests received at a suburban church recently were cries for help from a congregation that's probably not a whole lot different from most. One woman had written, "My husband says he knows it's wrong, but he's leaving me. He says he doesn't feel the love he once did for me."

Another said, "Please pray for our teenage son, who is having problems with drugs."

Another one: "We have a beautiful home and plenty of money, but our family is falling apart. Help!"[1]

James Dobson, internationally renowned Christian psychologist, printed in his monthly magazine back in January of 1990 an article entitled "New Course for a New Decade." The author, Bob Welch, challenged today's Christian family to not let the decade leading to the new millennium become an extension of the Me Decade (of the '70s and '80s) but instead to herald the arrival of a new era: The We Decade. Families. Together. "Not statistical families who share the same roof, but husbands and wives who love each other more than anything else. And children who can turn to a parent, not some toll-free 1-800 hot line when they need to talk."[2]

This is a particularly challenging statement, especially when we consider some of the staggering statistics from the U.S. Census Bureau describing our society, statistics that give rise to prayer requests like the ones just mentioned. In the last twenty years, the marriage rate has fallen 30 percent while the divorce rate has risen 50 percent. Two of every five women giving birth to their first child were not married when they became pregnant. As a result, divorce and out-of-wedlock births have fueled an enormous increase in single-parent families: Nearly one in four children lives with a single parent.

According to the Family Research Council, slightly more than half of females and nearly two-thirds of males have had sexual intercourse by their eighteenth birthday. Birth rates among teens are nearly one-quarter higher now than in 1986. In 1996, 1 million children were victims of child abuse and neglect, with 1,077 dying as a result.

Every 17.3 minutes someone commits suicide in the United States. Suicide is the third leading cause of death among people ages fifteen to twenty-four. Every seventy-eight seconds a teenager attempts suicide, and every ninety minutes one succeeds. This is quite a picture of the family in these days!

What an awesome responsibility to be a parent! A secular psychologist notes that the qualities and attitudes of the parents are the most potent conditioning factors in the life of the child. What a sobering thought! But somehow hearing a statement like that only makes us feel worse at times, doesn't it? We say to ourselves, "I know I'm not the perfect parent. I blow it all the time. What hope is there for our family?"

Dr. Ross Campbell, in his book *How to Really Love Your Child*, reveals a significant statistic that helps put this in perspective: Because of the congenital temperaments of children, some children will automatically be easy children and others, difficult. Consequently, based upon those temperaments, 25 percent of children will have somewhat more negative than positive experiences in life no matter what; 25 percent of children will have somewhat more positive than negative experiences no matter what; how the other 50 percent experience life will be primarily determined by parental influence, whether the parents are nurturing, loving, and accepting or not.[3]

In other words, none of us can look at anyone else and judge the quality of their parenting by how the children turn out. As Dr. Graham Maxwell, professor of theology at Loma Linda University, reminded pastors and their wives in a seminar several years ago, even God, the perfect parent, lost a third of His children in heaven.

But with that disclaimer in mind, let's take a look at a story of incredible contrast. It describes the power of family influence. Notice the dynamics of this story in the context of one of the most significant factors relating to what it means to be a real Sabbath keeper. As we reflect on this story, we must ask ourselves the questions, "What does it take to provide those around me with an environment conducive to their growth, and am I doing the best I can with what God has given me? What does this have to say about what it means to be a real Sabbath keeper, how do you play heaven with the family?"

2 Chronicles 22 says that the next king to come to Judah's throne after Jehoram was Ahaziah. He was Jehoram's youngest son, twenty-two years old, when the people made him king. But he was not a good king—he did all the bad things Ahab of Israel did, like Baal worship involving immorality and prostitution, abuse of the people, and rebellion against God. Why does he turn out this way? If we look carefully at the story, we can discover some clues.

The chronicler makes it clear in verse 3 that Ahaziah turned out this way because of his parents' influence. Notice the kind of home atmosphere Ahaziah grows up in. While still a young boy, he witnessed the brutal murder of his cousins, uncles, and aunts by his father because his father felt insecure about his position as king. Imagine what that would be like.

And then some years later, when the Palestinian and Arab raiders invaded the land, he watched his father bargain away his brothers and their families to save his own neck. They ended up dying too. But he, Ahaziah, was miraculously saved because the raiders didn't think he was worth worrying about.

So how would these childhood experiences make Ahaziah feel? He had grown up in an atmosphere of no security—he had come to see that his parents' love was conditional. "If I don't get in their way, maybe they'll love and accept me. My uncles and aunts, and even my brothers, weren't valuable enough for my parents to want them around. How could I be, either? Even the invaders didn't think I was worth much!"

His mother was Athaliah, Jezebel's daughter. It was obvious she didn't care for him, or anyone else for that matter, except herself. Later, when she heard that Ahaziah had been killed by Jehu, rather than mourn for him, she proceeded to destroy his whole family to consolidate her power.

With these kinds of parental patterns, is it any wonder that Ahaziah grew up feeling totally insecure about his parents' love. And since parents have the strongest influence in the formation of their children's picture of God, no wonder Ahaziah readily rebelled against God. "God is like my parents. I'm never secure with their love, so how can I be with God's love? I can never measure up for Him either, so why try? If that's the way God is, I don't want any part of Him!"

So the chronicler says in verse 3, Ahaziah "walked in the ways of the house of Ahab, for his mother encouraged him in doing wrong." We all desperately need the approval and affection of our parents. In some way or another, we'll do what it takes to get it—or if we can't get it from them, we'll try to find that approval and affection from someone or somewhere else.

Ahaziah found himself drawn to his uncle Joram, his mother's brother, who was the king of Israel. Perhaps Ahaziah was looking to him as the father he no longer had. He needed approval and acceptance. But that relationship with his evil uncle only made things worse for Ahaziah. He went farther down the road to rebellion against God and ultimately to his untimely death. He was only twenty-two years old. He had been king less than a year.

Ahaziah's life was a tragic demonstration of the power of parental patterns and influence.

But notice now an incredible contrast to Ahaziah's story. It concerns his son Joash, whose story begins in the few remaining verses of 2 Chronicles 22.

When the wicked queen mother, Athaliah, saw that her son the king was dead, rather than mourn for him, she immediately proceeded to destroy his whole royal family. Can you imagine that? This lady was so cold, if she ever bled, she'd bleed icicles.

But into this ugly scene came two of the Bible's great heroes: Jehosheba and her husband Jehoiada. Snatching Ahaziah's one-year-old son, Joash, from the very arms of violent death, they rushed the boy and his nurse into the inner sanctum of the sanctuary. They kept him hidden there from the wicked queen for six long years.

Who was this couple that risked their lives for six years to save and nurture this royal son? Amazingly, the woman Jehosheba was King Ahaziah's sister. This woman had grown up with the same parents as Ahaziah, in the same atmosphere. She may have struggled with the same feelings of insecurity.

Perhaps it was the high priest Jehoiada who helped her to break out of the trap of evil that her brother fell into. Perhaps it was his love that helped her to see herself as valuable to God and to see her nephew Joash as precious to God as well—too precious to let die to serve his grandmother's selfish purposes.

When the crisis came and the massacre began, she and her husband risked their lives to save her brother's son. And for the next six years, they willingly put their necks on the line every day to give their royal nephew a safe sanctuary in the church.

In spite of the fact that Joash was the son of Ahaziah, the evil king, and grandson of Athaliah, the wicked queen mother, he emerged from his hiding six years later completely opposite from them all. Why such a change?

What a different atmosphere Joash grew up in. Though he never had his parents, he had an uncle and aunt, his adopted parents, whom he knew cared about him. For six years they revealed to him a love that was willing to give and to risk life itself no matter what! Joash grew up with the security of knowing he was loved and accepted. Every day he saw Jehosheba and Jehoiada risk their lives for him. As he grew older, he began to sense the reality of what they were doing for him. He felt valuable and full of worth.

Because Jehoiada was the priest, Joash grew up connecting God with his loving uncle. What Jehoiada said about God, he lived. Confined to the safe recesses of the sanctuary, his aunt and uncle must have spent a lot of time with him, nurturing his sense of worth and value, painting for him a picture of a God who loves His children.

All of this took place to such an extent that when this seven-year-old emerged from his hiding and was crowned king, he became one of the great spiritual reformers in Judah's history. What a contrast to his father's story—a positive testimony to the power of family influence.

What were some of the factors that made such a difference in these two stories? Parents/loved ones willing to take the time to deliberately nurture an atmosphere of warmth and acceptance, approval and affirmation. Two significant elements: time and quality attention.

Nancy Van Pelt, in her book *The Compleat Parent,* lists the ten most desirable qualities for fathers stated by a group of 369 high school boys and 415 girls. Do you know the quality for fathers that was most desirable to these kids, that received the most votes: "spending time with his kids."[4]

In contrast, though, according to another study done by a psychologist on 300 seventh- and eighth-grade boys, the boys were asked to keep a diary of the time in an average week that their fathers spent with them. The typical father and son were alone seven and one-fourth minutes in an average week! Seven and one-fourth minutes!

In a survey by the American Sociological Review, working women said they talked with their husbands an average of twelve minutes each day. How can family members connect with each other if they don't stop long enough to concentrate on each other?

What's the key? Time. In the last few decades, convenience has become a way of life, often so we could have more time. We could pop a frozen entree in the microwave, withdraw money from a cash machine, program a computer to carry out our commands—all in seconds. In a sense, all these conveniences brought us closer to the yuppieized thirst for instant gratification.

But did all this bring us closer together as families? Not often enough! Why? Because intimate and meaningful relationships cannot be popped into a microwave oven and zapped to life. Meaningful family relationships are the product of years of nurturing, seasons of sacrifice, months of sometimes mundane attention, and weeks of Sabbaths—time.

This is why the Sabbath is so absolutely vital. As Marva Dawn emphasizes, one of the greatest gifts of Sabbath keeping is its gift of time.

> There is no need for any rush, no pressure to get rid of guests after awhile in order to get some work done. Instead, the gift of time to explore at a leisurely pace promotes carefulness, discovery, and plumbing the depths of relationships.[5]

Time. Sabbath time. The number one characteristic of real Sabbath keepers is their deliberate, intentional use of time in the middle of hundred-mile-an-hour living to foster relationships, beginning with God and then the family relationships. Time. Sabbath time. Playing heaven with the family is structuring time to bring the qualities of heaven into the life of the family now.

That's why George Bernard Shaw, even clear back at the turn of the century, made the statement, "Save the Sabbath and it will go a long way toward saving the family."[6]

How does this work? Here's the way Herbert Saunders views it:

> The Sabbath, if it is to have any meaning for us, beyond mere formalism, must be shared. Such sharing begins at home. The Sabbath is the family's day. . . . It is a time for the renewal of family ties and personal relationships so often lost throughout the week. It is a time to relate more closely to the needs of each individual family member and to share experiences which are often lost in the maze of everyday living. . . . [In this age] there is so little time when family shares anything. A sincere and cooperative keeping of the Sabbath will restore some of the needed family solidarity, and may preserve our society."[7]

Sabbath keeping, playing heaven, begins in the home, with family members taking TIME with each other. The greatest gift God has given us is His willingness to spend time with us. His unfathomable willingness to step out of eternity and into our human time in human form to be with us in human flesh—Immanuel, God With Us.

I call this the incarnational principle of Sabbath keeping: entering into the individual worlds of our loved ones in ways meaningful to them, so they can enjoy the qualities of heaven with us. Incarnational Sabbath keeping is playing heaven with the family.

Even so, this is one of the greatest gifts we can give our families. True Sabbath keeping is taking time off from something else in order to make time for someone else. A young man, whose father was a world-famous Seventh-day Adventist church leader, told a friend how proud he was of his father. His pride was obvious as he so eagerly talked about all the great things his dad had done—for other people.

And then he said, "But he never had time for me." The young

man's dejection was written all over his face. That hits pretty close to home!

The beauty of true Sabbath keeping is that it gives us time for quality relationships by taking away from us a part of the time we spend on other "everyday" activities. This is why Sabbath keeping, by necessity, must involve setting aside or a refusal to engage in many normal weekly activities that would detract from the building and nurturing of our family relationships.

A commitment to not work on the Sabbath, for example, or to not go shopping on the Sabbath, or whatever else it is that we normally have to do in the week that tends to separate family members or consume our individual energies—a commitment to intentionally put aside those kinds of things is not legalism—it's true love!

Affection takes time. In the mad rush of our society's pace, everything gets turned backwards. People jump into bed together to get to know one another instead of choosing committed sexual communion as the culmination of a long process of establishing intimacy on many other levels. The Christian community as an alternative society can promote social intimacy in various dimensions of life by offering opportunities for Sabbath fellowship in worship, meals, activities, programs, and possibilities for service. We as individuals can choose to spend our time building careful intimacy with friends and relatives through sharing our deepest thoughts and feelings, giving gifts, and doing favors for each other, as well as through gentle touches, enfolding hugs and tender kisses."[8]

Affection, intimacy, the nurturing of relationships take time. So God graciously gives us the gift of the Sabbath to help us. *And since Sabbath keeping is a lifestyle, true Sabbath keepers are characterized by their deliberate and intentional attempts to build TIME for family relationships throughout the week, not just on one day.*

Ludwig Koehler's statement is particularly challenging and stirring: "Before God's throne there will hardly ever be a greater testimony given on your behalf than the statement, 'He had time for me.' "[9]

But obviously it's not just the amount of time we spend with our families that counts. It's also the quality of that time. Athaliah spent a lot of time counseling her son in wrong ways. Joash's uncle and aunt no doubt spent a lot of time, too, but in nurturing an atmosphere of love and approval. The results were worlds apart.

One of the Gallup organization's recent decade studies of America's youth revealed some interesting dynamics. The top three topics that teens would like to discuss more with their parents were family finances, drugs, and drinking, in that order. That corresponds to what teens say are the top two biggest problems facing them: Drug and alcohol abuse.

But according to this survey, could you guess the top two topics that teens say their parents spend the most time arguing with them about? Keeping their room clean and clothes and appearance. Drinking and drugs are clear at the bottom of that list.[10] I'm not sure things have changed much in recent years.

Somehow or other we're not matching the time with the needs. We need incarnational Sabbath keeping (like God models with us): entering into each other's worlds to enable each other to experience the qualities of heaven in ways that are meaningful to each other.

It's so easy as a parent, when experiencing frustration, to major on minors. We have to constantly examine ourselves by asking, "Is the time I spend with my children quality time, being sensitive to their needs, hearing and responding to their often nonverbal cries for attention? Am I doing my best to use whatever resources I can, like the Sabbath, to nurture an atmosphere in my home of unqualified love and affirmation? Am I playing heaven with my family?"

Billy Graham tells a story about a college girl who was critically injured in a car accident. As she lay dying, she said to her mother, "Mom, you taught me everything I needed to know to get by in life—how to light my cigarette, how to hold my cocktail glass, how to have sex without getting pregnant. But you never taught me how to die. Teach me quick, Mom, 'cuz I'm dying."

How tragic it would be to fail to spend quality time nurturing our children in the most important areas of life! A Seattle high school girl observed at her commencement address that people wonder why there are so many one-parent homes, why so many parents are abandoning their children, why the increase in physical and sexual abuse of children. Why is there the need for drug and alcohol treatment centers? Why has the number of family and adolescent therapists skyrocketed?

And then she mused, "What has happened to long walks and longer talks, going to church on Sunday, and eating dinner at Grandma and Grandpa's house?"

Sabbath time—playing heaven with the family—has it been lost? Can we regain it? Do we have the courage to be deliberate and intentional about our Sabbath keeping with our families, regardless of the costs of time and effort?

Yet the reality is that even if parents did it perfectly, some children would rebel against it. As Dr. Maxwell said, even God, the perfect parent, lost a third of His children in heaven.

So why try? But as Maxwell went on to say, let's make sure that if our children ever reject God, they're rejecting the right picture of God. So we must commit ourselves to really playing heaven with our families—using the power of our influence to nurture an atmosphere in our homes that portrays a God who loves and affirms without qualifications, who values us so much that He willingly risked His life for us just to spend time with us, to live with us, to give Himself to us. That is real incarnational Sabbath keeping! That is playing heaven with the family!

Chapter 12

Playing Heaven With the Homeless

Jack Draper has been out of work for three months, and now it looks like his mill will not ever need him again—or any of the 150 others laid off by the iron and steel mill. Jack and Kitty have been faithful members of the church for six years. He has served on the board twice, and she's been a teacher in the children's division for three years running. Now they're asking for financial help. Should the church do something?

Tina Edwards has just begun attending church with her infant daughter. Her parents have kicked her out, the child's father will not marry her, and she hasn't yet made a profession of faith. But she needs help as an unwed teenage mother. Should the church do something?

David and Merlene Olshausen are in their seventies. He's tried to find work, but no one will hire him at his age. Merlene is confined to bed with crippling arthritis. Their Social Security payments cover the rent, but not much more; their children don't seem to care. The elders at the church want to help, but David's too proud to accept charity. Should the church do something?[1]

Worldwide, 200 million people are currently estimated to be victims of slavery, 127 years after the Emancipation Proclamation, according to the *World Monitor.* Should the church do something?

Western nations donate roughly $200 million per year in aid to developing nations to help them prevent AIDS and care for its victims. This is roughly the amount the world spends on weapons of war every two hours. It's estimated that annually, 54,000 people will die from AIDS around the world. With proper information and education, as many as 12-14,000 of these people could be saved from death by AIDS.

Although in the United States, death from AIDS has declined in the last several years, pushing the disease out of the top ten causes of death, there are still some 40,000 new infections every year. This means that more people are living with and potentially spreading AIDS and the virus that causes it. And doctors worry that the wonder-drug combinations that have been so successful will eventually stop working.

In 1990, Neal C. Wilson, former president of the General Conference of Seventh-day Adventists, wrote that on the basis of statistical studies, it is estimated that in the near future, in many countries of the world, every church congregation numbering 100 or more will include at least one member who has a friend or relative with AIDS. Should the church do something?

Roughly one-fourth of the world's population—1.2 billion people—cannot afford the basic necessities of food, clothing, and shelter. Perhaps two-thirds of these "poorest of the poor" are under the age of fifteen. More than ten thousand people starve to death every day, with thousands more going blind annually because of dietary deficiency.

We don't even have to look beyond our shores to find the need. A shocking 9.7 million Americans live in rural pockets of poverty similar to Third World poverty.[2] In the 320 poorest counties in the

United States, child mortality rates are 45 percent higher than the national average. That means twenty children out of one thousand do not survive their first few years—that's a child survival rate comparable to Panama's.

In Laredo, Texas, for example, 25 million gallons of raw sewage are pumped daily into the Rio Grande River. People aren't allowed to swim in that water, but they hoist it out by bucketfuls and drink it, bathe in it, and wash their clothes in it. It's the only water available to them.

In the Appalachian mountains of Tennessee, families live with no electricity, running water, or indoor plumbing. In some areas there, more than half of the high school students drop out. Should the church do something about all this poverty at home and abroad?

Throughout the United States, the most significant single change in the modern family is the increasing commonness of two working parents. Most families find it necessary to have two incomes. While child care costs the average working mother's family 6 percent of its income, the 1.6 million working mothers who live below the poverty level spent an average of 22 percent of their family's income on child care. At the same time, federal support has either declined or failed to keep pace with the escalating burdens. Should the church do something?

Drunk drivers cause a disabling injury every minute and kill an innocent victim every twenty-two minutes. More than one million crashes every year are drug-or alcohol-related, with one-third of the annual deaths taking place in the fourteen to twenty-four-year-old age group. Should the church do something?

Let's face it, we live in a world and in an age when human need is at its greatest. Everywhere we look, if our eyes are sensitive to it, we see people who are hurting.

Three psychiatrists sometime back stated that acute loneliness was the most dangerous and widespread illness in America. It was affecting from 75 to 90 percent of all Americans. Loneliness from what? Separation and isolation brought about by the death of a loved one, divorce, moving to a new place and having to face new people, new work associates, new kids at a new school, losing a friend, being single, experiencing marital problems. Has it changed much in recent years?

We don't have to look very far to see people who are lonely, hurting, and in need. In his book *The Pursuit of Loneliness*, Philip Slater suggests that the growth of social fragmentation is so severe in the United States that it is pushing our culture to the breaking point.

So, should the church do something? Does it even have an obligation to intervene in the pain of humanity all around us? After all, say some people, if we spend our time on social issues, we'll be missing valuable time to prepare ourselves for the Second Coming. Being ready for the time of trouble is more important anyway, isn't it? After all, when Jesus finally returns, the world and everything in it will be destroyed anyway. So why bother trying to stem the tide of pain and suffering now? Better to concentrate on the eternal and spiritual issues.

Does being a Sabbath keeper have anything to do with such overwhelming needs? As we've looked at Sabbath keeping revolving around the experience of "playing heaven," that is, deliberately attempting to bring the qualities and values of heaven into the present, how does this work with the needs just mentioned in this section? Does it apply? How do we "play heaven with the homeless," those disenfranchised, needy, lonely people all around us?

I'd like to suggest a model that will provide some guiding principles in answering those questions: Jesus' three-step model of Sabbath keeping. It's found in a story recorded in Luke 14:1-6.

The day is Sabbath. Jesus is invited by a prominent Pharisee to a sumptuous Sabbath meal. He goes, along with numerous other dignitaries there by invitation, of course. This is a big affair!

Jesus looks around the dimly lighted room. The table has been set with an incredible spread of wonderful-smelling food. His eyes are still getting accustomed to the dark so, as He moves toward the table, He practically runs into something. Looking down, he notices the figure of a man right in front of Him who's strangely out of place in the midst of such a pretentious gathering. Jesus' gaze rests compassionately on him.

Suddenly, the whole room gets very silent—all small "committees" stop. All eyes are fixed upon this duo in the center of the room. The guests are eyeing Jesus with suspicion and looking upon this man with revulsion.

You see, the man is suffering from dropsy, a most embarrassingly uncomfortable condition. The body tissues become swollen from a buildup of surplus fluid causing various extremities of the body to become bloated and oversized, like the feet or the legs or the face. Definitely it's not a condition you'd like to have while being the center of attention at a special banquet for dignitaries!

So why is this man here? Because the Pharisees like him? Because they think he's great to have around? Because these theologians think he has a worthwhile contribution to make to their theological discussions on Sabbath?

No, he's brought there by one of the Pharisees, torn from the privacy and safe refuge of his home, to be used—not for the good of medical science, not for the good of theological reflection, but to trap Jesus, to give them something for which to condemn Jesus.

Knowing all of this and still unintimidated, Jesus, standing there beside this grotesque figure of a man, poses a question to the preachers and theologians looking on. "All right, you men are experts in the law, you pride yourselves on your grasp of the intricacies of legalities. Tell me, what does the law say about healing on the Sabbath? Is that in harmony with God's intent for Sabbath keeping?"

A few Sabbaths earlier, in front of the whole church, no less, Jesus had posed a similar question to the Pharisees, as He stood beside a man with a shriveled-up hand: "Which is lawful on the Sabbath," he had asked them, "to do good or to do evil, to save life or to destroy it?" These are fundamental questions when it comes to understanding God's plan for Sabbath keeping.

So how do the preachers, lawyers, and theologians respond to Jesus' question? They choose to remain silent. According to their interpretation of the law, healing and ministry to the needy can only be performed on the Sabbath if it's a life or death situation. It's not allowed for chronic cases or situations that can just as well wait until sundown.

So in the face of Jesus' question, they feel their interpretations to be most inadequate. After all, who in their right mind is going to answer a question like that by shouting out, "Yes, the Sabbath is a day for doing harm and destroying life! It is not lawful to do good on the Sabbath!" So instead, they choose to remain silent.

Looking down at the man who sits at His feet, Jesus dares to do three things to him:

(1) TOUCH. Jesus takes hold of him. He deliberately touches him. Imagine what that does to this man who has been shunned as ugly and avoided as sinful. Jesus' touch begins to renew his self-concept—he starts feeling like a man again.

(2) INVOLVE. Jesus heals him. He involves Himself with this man's real needs. To this suffering man, this healing will forever have double significance. He experiences physical restoration. The ugliness disappears. He can go anywhere now without being stared at and laughed at. His sense of guilt and spiritual uncleanness forced upon him by the destructive traditions of the Pharisees are gone. He can stand tall now without being looked down upon by others—he is free and clean in Jesus!

(3) PROTECT. Jesus sends the new man away for his own protection—away from the people there who might try to enslave him again with guilt and shame, who might rebuke him for breaking the Sabbath and so bring sorrow to a *day* that should now be spent in joyful celebration. With everything He's done to him, Jesus has protected the man's self-respect. What do you think this man's attitude toward the Sabbath and toward God will be from now on?

With the center of attention now gone, Jesus turns to the Pharisees and guests and makes His point: "If one of you has a son or an ox that falls into a well on the Sabbath day, will you not immediately pull him out?"

And for the second time, the preachers, lawyers, and theologians are reduced to silence. Why? Because they've been confronted with the pettiness of their priorities: They would save their own sons or oxen from danger or harm on the Sabbath because both are so important to the status of their lives—a son for heritage sake and oxen for economic security. But when it comes to meeting human needs for the sake of human needs, that can't be done on the Sabbath! They have mixed-up priorities.

Jesus directs their attention beyond their petty rules to the fundamental principle of Sabbath keeping: Not to save life is in fact to take it; not to do that which enhances life is in fact to diminish life.

Jesus reveals a God who values the kind of worship from His people that refuses to be separated from the realities and needs of life—a God who made the Sabbath as an experience that safeguards the value of life, that enhances the quality and celebration of life.

Notice what Ellen White says in *The Desire of Ages:*

> God could not for a moment stay His hand, or man would faint and die. [So] man also has a work to perform on this day [of the Sabbath.] The necessities of life must be attended to, the sick must be cared for, the wants of the needy must be supplied. He will not be held guiltless who neglects to relieve suffering on the Sabbath. God's holy rest day was made for man, and acts of mercy are in perfect harmony with its intent. God does not desire His creatures to suffer an hour's pain that may be relieved upon the Sabbath or any other day.[3]

If, as true Sabbath keepers, we were to take this concept seriously, it might mean doing things we have perhaps traditionally felt uncomfortable doing—especially on the Sabbath. Richard Davidson, chairman of the Old Testament Department at the Seventh-day Adventist Theological Seminary, in Berrien Springs, Michigan, tells the following story related to him by a pastor-friend.

In a district in the South, the local Seventh-day Adventist church had few members and little influence in the community. So the pastor held an evangelistic series, and not a single nonmember showed up.

But about that time a newly converted Adventist plumber moved into the community. The man didn't have the necessary qualifications to give Bible studies or participate in singing bands—but he was an excellent plumber.

So every Sabbath afternoon, he loaded his tools in the back of his pickup truck and set off down the road. He stopped at every place where it looked like someone really needy might be living—the poor, the widows, the disabled, etc. Then he simply asked if they had any plumbing that needed fixing.

After he completed the job and the person he had helped asked how much he wanted, the plumber replied, "No charge! This is God's gift to you on His holy Sabbath."

Sabbath after Sabbath— throughout the town—he made his statement, "This is God's gift to you on His holy Sabbath."

When the church had an evangelistic series the next year, there was standing room only. It seemed as if the whole town had shown up, eager to learn about the plumber's God and His Sabbath.

True Sabbath keeping means "playing heaven," deliberately and intentionally attempting to bring the qualities and values of heaven into the present, not just for our own lives but for the "homeless" as well, those disenfranchised, lonely, hurting, needy people all around us. Sabbath keeping, "playing heaven with the homeless," means refusing to neglect to relieve suffering wherever it can be found.

Sakae Kubo points out that the Sabbath not only reminds us of our deliverance, but it commands us to extend the blessing to those under oppression or servitude. It's not enough "to rejoice in and enjoy one's own salvation. One must also work with God to bring deliverance [to the needy everywhere]. . . . Sabbath observance has integral social and humanitarian aspects that we dare not forget."[4]

So what can we do, as Sabbath keepers, to "play heaven with the homeless?" The needs are so overwhelming when we stop and look at them that sometimes it's easier to throw up our hands in despair and give up before we even start. But starting somewhere, however small it may be, is at least a start.

Let me suggest following Jesus' three-step model that we saw earlier of how to meet needs: (1) Touch, (2) Involve, and (3) Protect.

(1) TOUCH. If there's anything lonely, hurting, disenfranchised people need from us it's a loving, gentle touch that communicates warmth, solidarity, and caring—an arm around the shoulder, a firm handshake, a hug. Giving money is so much easier sometimes, but it's impersonal too. People need touch and human contact.

People who've contracted various diseases, for example, especially those diseases that are looked down on by others or produce fear in people and are terminal, like AIDS or cancer, need the warmth and caring of human touch. Why not call the local hospital or state or local health department or even the National AIDS hotline for information on where the nearest support programs are and on how to help?

Why not contact a person or family who has recently lost a loved one and provide a loving arm or listening ear?

Like Fannidell Peeples of Detroit, Michigan.[5] Born with scoliosis, a disabling spinal disease, Peeples was orphaned at seven and spent much of her childhood in foster homes. "I cried for years," she says. "Then I came to understand that the worst place to be is with someone who doesn't love you."

She never married, and when physical woes kept her from fully using her teaching degree, she began baby-sitting. In 1983, she volunteered to become an unpaid helper at Children's Hospital, in Detroit.

The "Peep," as nurses lovingly call this sixty-nine-year-old woman, has chosen a mission that many regular staffers find difficult: to comfort babies about to succumb to drug withdrawal, AIDS, or other diseases.

"I stroke and I care and I rock as they're on their way out," she says. "I tell them, 'I love you and I'll miss you.' They've missed so many things. We owe them the dignity to leave as human beings at least." Step 1—TOUCH.

(2) INVOLVE. That means going to where the needs are, getting ourselves actively involved in some way. For example, there are churches in Washington, D.C., which have chosen to link together in trying to do something about the drug and alcohol epidemic.

Not only do they help financially, but part of the program involves volunteering for three-hour "after-school" tutorials and skill-development sessions with groups of twenty children at each site. The children are helped with homework and shown how to cope with problems at home, school, and with peers.

When I pastored in Auburn, Washington, the Auburn Coalition on Teenage Pregnancy Prevention, in conjunction with Big Sisters of King County, began a training program for Auburn women to become mentors to girls from ages six to thirteen. They were seeking to provide the girls an opportunity to see positive role models and build friendships with adults. It's an attempt to do something constructive and preventive with the high number of teenage pregnancies in Auburn (which at that time had the highest percentage in King County).

Our church hosted the first training program by providing our facilities free of charge. Why not volunteer to be a Big Sister to help with this growing need in so many communities?

Why not call the State Patrol, for example, and ask how you can become involved with the activities of groups like Mothers Against Drunk Drivers and other volunteer organizations that work to prevent alcohol-related accidents?

One of the major news magazines reported about an inner city church that got so fed up with alcohol and smoking advertisements on billboards in their community targeted specifically to young people that they decided to whitewash the billboards.

Their anger is well-founded. According to the Centers for Disease Control and Prevention, the number of American youths taking up smoking as a daily habit jumped 73 percent between R. J. Reynolds Tobacco Company's Joe Camel advertisement campaign debut in 1988 and 1996. The CDC believes that those kid-friendly cartoon tobacco ads are partly to blame.

Naturally, those inner-city churches' response created quite a stir with the advertisers and the community. But if that might be too radical an activity, why not take the offensive and at least try renting a billboard in town and advertising against alcohol and drugs? Why not, as a church, sponsor a stop-smoking program targeted to teenagers?

Why not do something tangible like getting involved with a local soup and sandwich ministry to the homeless? Why not do something as simple as putting food baskets together for needy families this Thanksgiving and Christmas? Or call a community service center about how you can help with clothing or food needs (Seventh-day Adventist churches in most cities have a local community service center and would welcome help or volunteers).

What about calling Adventist Development and Relief Agency (ADRA), headquartered in Silver Spring, Maryland, and asking how you can help with disaster, hunger, and poverty relief around the world? Perhaps it might involve taking a vacation somewhere to help dig wells, build homes, distribute food. Perhaps it might involve financially sponsoring an overseas child or even becoming a pen pal. There are scores of ways, small and big, to get involved in helping meet the needs of people all over the world.

When Ion Berindei, who in 1969 escaped the horrors of the Ceausescu Romanian regime and now lives in Medford, Massachusetts, heard about abused children in Romania's state-run orphanages, he went to investigate. What he found defied imagination. "There was this incredible stench," he says. "Children lying in their own waste. When I saw them, I gave them what they wanted—hugs."[6]

With the help of a Romanian cinematographer, he traveled 1,800 miles in ten days to videotape conditions in fifteen orphanages and three children's hospitals. ABC's *20/20* news program included a portion of his tapes in an October telecast. The network received more than 30,000 letters about the children, the most ever on one segment.

"Most of the children in the worst shape not only are adopted," said 20/20's Tom Jarriel, "but have been adopted out of the piece."

Brindei continues his work. While his wife works as a part-time professor at Tufts University, Berindei puts in fifteen-hour days on the orphans' behalf. He says, "I have discovered a quality for giving inside myself that I didn't know I had."

Like Beth and S.T. Johnson Jr.[7] Earning $85,000 between the two of them, they had it made. After their first child, they found out they couldn't have any more. When S.T. III turned eleven, they decided to adopt. So arrived Jeff, Charles, and Greg into their family—the only adopted identical triplets in the U.S.

Born nine weeks prematurely to an alcoholic mother and a drug addict father, the boys were considered impossible to place unless they were split up. Despite warnings from her own pediatrician, who told her, "Don't do it . . . your life will be chaos!" Beth was undeterred.

"The boys were basically unwanted," she says. "I didn't want to see them end up at an adoption fair, like something in a Dickens novel."

After the boys' arrival in 1986, the pediatrician's prediction largely came true. Because of their prenatal exposure to alcohol, the triplets all required speech therapy and suffered from sporadic febrile seizures during which they stopped breathing (like all three did in a single weekend, once).

So Beth, S.T., and their first son S.T. III all took turns on what they called "seizure patrol" each night, sleeping on the triplets' bedroom floor to keep watch over them.

Beth had to quit her job to care for the boys, and growing medical bills (over twenty thousand dollars in the first few years) forced the family to put their home up for sale. But do they have regrets? No!

"I'll never stop loving them," Beth says. "The three boys asked me once if they grew in my tummy. I told them, 'No, you grew in my heart.' "

Like Dr. Anne Brooks, the soft-spoken nun and osteopath who has forsaken a much more lucrative medical career to work in Tutwiler, Mississippi, in the heart of America's deepest poverty.[8] The average annual household income is $9,300. In addition to seeing about six hundred patients a month, her clinic offers counseling, literacy and general equivalency diploma classes, child care, summer programs for children, a thrift shop, and field trips for senior citizens.

Daily she confronts seemingly intolerable lives with grace, humor, and dignity. "These people live in situations where I would be so depressed I'd probably go hang myself. They give me much more than I give them."

In Tutwiler, sewage empties into the bayou, which floods. "Last year it flooded five times," she says. "I've had people in the hospital because of it." There are people who won't go to their outhouses because of the snakes and the rats. Rats will be on the rafters, in the kitchen, in people's homes.

"I've had people whose toes have been eaten off by rats at night. People shouldn't have to live that way. This is America. We have the technology and we have the money," says Dr. Anne with indignation.

Yet with patience and acceptance, in her quiet and loving way, Dr. Brooks is making a difference in a little corner of the world. "You learn that perhaps you can't change the whole world all at once," she says with a smile. But she stays to make a difference.

In her book *The Desire of Ages,* again Ellen White says: "It is the service of love that God values. . . . The gospel places a high value upon humanity as the purchase of the blood of Christ, and it teaches a tender regard for the wants and woes of man. . . . We should neglect nothing that will tend to benefit a human being."[9] Step 2—INVOLVE.

Finally, (3) PROTECT. Jesus showed extreme sensitivity to that disfigured man's self-esteem by protecting him from his accusers. He treated the man with real respect. After healing him, He sent him away from his accusers.

How easy it is when we help people, to come across as though we're really doing them a favor, patronizing them, like we're serving down rather than serving up.

For example, Delores Curran, quoted in *The Christian Speaker's Treasury*, observed recently that because many adolescents feel ugly and unlovable most of the time, they need constant reassurance that they're attractive and loved.

> I remember particularly the great number of teenage girls I taught in high school who were never made aware of their unique and appealing traits, such as an engaging smile, a special zest, or a keen wit. But they knew about their acne or their extra five pounds, and that was all that counted.[10]

What a need there is for us simply to reassure people of every generation, to build them up, to protect their self-respect. How we talk and relate to the people we help makes a world of difference in how they feel about our help. Step 3—PROTECT.

One dictionary defines kindness as "the state of being sympathetic, gentle, friendly, tenderhearted, and generous." What a beautiful description of Jesus. And that is a description of true Sabbath keepers too.

We're all surrounded by the homeless—people in need of our kindness and generosity. There are lonely people in hospitals and nursing homes. Families struggling with financial difficulties need food, clothes, and cash for their rent. Elderly neighbors may be unable to till their gardens or shovel snow from their sidewalks. Those who are discouraged could be lifted up by a note or phone call. The new person at church would feel welcomed by an invitation to dinner. The single mother and her kids might be thrilled to be included in your family picnic or outing. The non-Christian couple down the block would be delighted to receive a jar of your freshly-made preserves.[11]

The list is endless, isn't it? But it always is for the Sabbath keeper, for the ones who choose to "play heaven with the homeless." True Sabbath keepers, who regularly experience the grace of God in their own lives, develop sensitive heart-eyes, grace-giving hands, to make a difference with the "homeless" people all around them. They're intentional about their giving lifestyle.

> One of the most important aspects of Sabbath keeping is that we embrace intentionality. That phrase emphasizes the value of taking care how we do what we do. . . . Such deliberateness goes against the grain of many Christian lives in twentieth-century America. We so easily fall into patterns and habits of the world around us in its outrageous lack of commitment that we rarely take time to consider how we do what we do. . . . Sabbath keeping says clearly that we are not going to do what everybody else does. We are going to be deliberate about our choices in order to live truly as we want to live in response to the grace of God. We are committed to certain values and, therefore, live in accordance with them as fully as we can.[12]

What makes Sabbath keepers so intentional about their lifestyles, even refusing not to become involved in spite of the personal risks? As Brennan Manning states so succinctly, "The more rooted we are in the love of God the more generously we live our faith and practice it."[13]

True Sabbath keepers, those who deliberately choose to "play heaven with the homeless," can live and love so generously because they, through the Sabbath are regularly reminded of God's grace, and they regularly experience that grace. And that grace empowers them to act graciously wherever there's a need!

The late Dawson Trotman, founder of The Navigators, was visiting Taiwan. During the visit he hiked with a Taiwanese pastor back into one of the mountain villages to meet with some of the national Christians. The roads and trails were wet, and their shoes became terribly muddy.

Later, someone asked this Taiwanese pastor what he remembered most about Dawson Trotman. Without hesitation the man replied, "He cleaned my shoes."

How surprised this humble national pastor must have been when he got up the next morning after their hike to find that the Christian leader from America had gotten up before him and cleaned the mud from his shoes.[14] "He cleaned my shoes."

That is Sabbath keeping at its best—playing heaven with the homeless!

Chapter 13

Playing Heaven With the Planet

A barge loaded with garbage travels from country to country and from port to port, looking for a place to dump it. Used medical syringes and hospital waste wash up on a metropolitan beach in the East. The media warns of AIDS contamination and infection (which later proves to be insupportable). Dead porpoises wash up on the Atlantic beaches. Someone theorizes that a virus is killing them, maybe even AIDS. Biologists reject the AIDS analogy. But when asked what is killing the porpoises, they say "Environmental stresses." In other words, the result of today's lifestyles.

Factories with belching smokestacks work around the clock to prepare all kinds of creature comforts we think we cannot do without—and in the process dump lethal toxic waste into our waterways. In the late 1960s, for example, Lake Erie (which in the previous decade had yielded seven million pounds of blue pike every year) became so polluted by industrial and domestic poisons that every living creature in it died.

In our country alone, about 142 million tons of smoke and noxious fumes are dumped into the atmosphere every year. Every ten minutes a four-engine jet aircraft emits two and two-third tons of carbon dioxide.

So what? Well, besides being poisonous to breathe, carbon dioxide is a major "greenhouse gas" that prevents solar radiation from escaping back into space and contributes to the global warming affecting this planet.

What's the effect? Typical of global warming scenarios was the 1988 drought which reduced China's grain crop by 3 percent, the Soviet Union's by 9 percent, and the United States' by 30 percent. The frightening fact of all this was that it left us, at that time, with only a sixty-day supply of surplus grain in the world.

What are we doing to our planet? The *Adventist Review* made this observation:

> If nature sings today, it is a mournful dirge. We have poisoned our world. Our materialistic madness is making earth uninhabitable for our children and succeeding generations. Our insatiable greed, our unquenchable lust for gadgets and things, our wanton consumerism are bleeding nature to death. And what kills nature kills us all.[1]

Do we as Sabbath keeping Christians have an obligation to help find a way out of this ecological nightmare—especially when we consider our strong belief in the soon coming of Jesus, knowing that things on earth not only will not get better but will in fact get worse? Does our eschatology preclude ecology? What should the true Sabbath keeper's response be to the environment? Can we really "play heaven" with the planet? How?

In Chapter 12 I alluded to the story in Luke 6:6-11. It provides a foundational principle that should help shape our response as Sabbath keepers to life on this planet. Jesus, the ultimate Sabbath keeper, gives us the example.

Jesus is teaching in the synagogue on this particular Sabbath. As usual, the scribes and Pharisees are spying on Jesus, looking for a reason to accuse and condemn Him, especially in connection with His Sabbath observance. The picture given here is that apparently these preachers have planted a man right up in the front of the congregation where Jesus will not be able to miss him. The man has a withered and deformed hand. It's paralyzed. The preachers are hoping Jesus will do something in public.

Sure enough! He doesn't disappoint them. Well aware of the situation, Jesus calls the man to come up front and stand beside Him in full view of the whole congregation. What a scene! All eyes follow him to the front. Anything that happens at this point is going to make a big impact.

Before doing anything, Jesus poses a question about lawfulness: " 'I ask you,' " He says, " 'which is lawful on the Sabbath: to do good or to do evil, to save life or to destroy it?' "

Jesus' piercing gaze sweeps over the expectant audience. Every eye is riveted upon Him and the deformed man. After waiting for His point to sink in, Jesus breaks the silence by acting in harmony with His principle. He says to the man, " 'Stretch out your hand.' "

Now, this is something that has been physically impossible for the man to do. Yet amazingly, the man responds obediently. People's heads and necks crane and stretch to see around pillars and other heads. In full view of everyone, the man begins flexing and moving his arm and hand in uncontrolled ecstasy. He's no longer paralyzed and deformed!

With that profound question and powerful act charging the worship atmosphere with electric commotion, Jesus provides us with the most fundamental principle of Sabbath keeping: not to save life is in fact to take it; not to do that which enhances life is in fact to diminish life.

True Sabbath keepers, in understanding the nature and meaning of the Sabbath, in following Jesus' example, always opt for life, choosing to bring relief to the suffering, choosing whatever it takes to enhance life on this planet, not diminish it. Jesus reveals a God who has a cosmic restoration program, who deliberately works to safeguard the value of life. His followers will embrace the same values.

We so often take these healing stories of Jesus and apply the principles only to our relationships with people. But we must remember that this very Jesus was not only the Son of man, He was the Son of God, the Creator God, incarnated in human flesh—the very Creator who in the beginning looked at all of His creative work; the heavens and firmament, earth's atmosphere, the sun, moon, and stars, the plants, flowers and trees, every creeping, crawling, swimming, flying creature in the seas, on the land and in the sky—He looked at all this He designed and brought into existence and said "It is good, very good!"

And then, creating man and woman, male and female human beings, created after His own likeness and in His own image, as He gave them the grand tour of Creation on that first Sabbath day, He said to them in essence, "This is our world. It's very good! I'm very proud of it! Take care of it for Me."

From the very beginning of life on this planet, as Jesus' example later shows, God places inherent value within all of created life. That's what the Sabbath is all about. As a memorial of Creation, it continually teaches us the inherent value of life—even in spite of sin.

Yes, sin has damaged creation. But the Sabbath is also a memorial of redemption—that God has a plan not only to redeem and restore people to His original image but also to restore all of creation to its rightful state.

As Dr. Bacchiocchi writes, "To accept God as the Creator and Restorer of the whole order means to be responsive to God's goals and intentions, by participating in His cosmic restoration program."[2]

So, as Jesus' example shows, true Sabbath keepers not only believe in the inherent value of all life, but they are actively involved in helping God restore life whenever and wherever possible.

This is why Albert Schweitzer said, "A man is ethical only when life, as such, is holy to him, that is, the lives of plants and animals as well as the lives of men. Moreover, he is ethical also only when he extends help to all life that is in need of it."[3]

The true Sabbath keeper treats nature with an overwhelming respect because God made it and so placed inherent value within it. We are fellow-creatures having come from the same hand of God.

But what about the command God gave to Adam and Eve to subdue and rule over creation? Does that imply a hierarchical order of existence, with people more valuable than the rest of nature? Are people to have dominion over nature?

In fact, through the centuries, many Christians have used the Genesis story to excuse their irresponsibility toward nature and justify its exploitation. John Stott tells about the author of books on otters, Gavin Maxwell, who once wrote about how he lost two lovely otter cubs he had brought back to Scotland from Nigeria.

One day, as he was out on the beach playing with his otters, a minister of the Church of Scotland, walking along the shore with a shotgun, found the two otters playing by the tide's edge. He shot them both. One was killed instantly, the other died of her wounds in the water.

When the minister found out what he had done, he expressed regret but then reminded the journalist, "The Lord gave man control over the beasts of the field. . . ."[4]

Attitudes and actions like this have led secular historians and scientists to place the blame for the ecological crisis on Christians. Lynn White, historian at UCLA, writes: "Christianity . . . not only established a dualism of man and nature, but also insisted that it is God's will that man exploit nature for his proper ends. . . . Christianity bears a huge burden of guilt."[5]

Unfortunately, there is a lot of truth in this accusation. But what a different perspective Jesus' life and Sabbath-keeping examples give.

"The distinctive Sabbath lifestyle, characterized not by the exploitation but by the admiration of the earth, not by the devastation of nature but by the exaltation of its Creator, provides a valuable model of responsible stewardship in an otherwise irresponsible society." "It teaches a person to view himself not as a predator but as a curator of God's creation." [6]

This was God's plan for human beings from the very beginning. Genesis 2:15 describes it: "The LORD God took the man and put him in the Garden of Eden to work it and take care of it."

What God charges Adam and Eve with is the responsibility of cultivation, not destruction of the earth. Human beings are stewards representing God on this planet.

Leviticus 25 describes God telling Israel, "You are but aliens and my tenants" (v. 23). So what does He go on to tell them? "Throughout the country that you hold as a possession, you must provide for the redemption of the land" (v. 24)—notice not just the redemption of people but also the redemption of the earth. God has a cosmic restoration program that involves not just human beings but also the planet. And as His tenants here, we are to be involved in that restoration process.

So what can we do? How can we "play heaven" with the planet? Let me suggest two significant principles. Each principle revolves around developing a basic attitude that in turn affects lifestyle: an attitude of respect for the planet and an attitude of admiration for creation.

1. An attitude of respect. The first thing we do to "play heaven" with the planet is to nurture an attitude of profound respect for all life, animate and inanimate, because it comes from the hand of God, as we do.

I'll never forget growing up as a child, living in Kobe, Japan, next door to another missionary family. One of the boys in that family used to beat up my brother and me every time he saw us step on an ant. In spite of the fact that we were black-and-blue more often than not, that made us so mad we went around stomping on ants to just make him mad. But as I've reflected about that experience, perhaps in a sense, he had a point (although his methodology was "misguided," as far as my bruised body was concerned).

Francis Schaeffer makes the point:

> We have the right to rid our houses of ants: but what we have no right to do is to forget to honor the ant as God made it, out in the place where God made the ant to be. When we meet the ant on the sidewalk, we step over him. He is a creature, like ourselves; not made in the image of God, it is true, but equal with man as far as creation is concerned. The ant and man are both creatures.[7]

However you might react to such a concept, the question is, what does it mean to be stewards and tenants for God on this planet? The first thing it means is to nurture an attitude of respect for all life that God has made. That is the bottom line.

The true Sabbath keeper must constantly walk the thin line between exercising dominion over nature and exploitation of nature. There are times when we have to use nature for our own survival or benefit. But exploitation, the misuse or abuse for the sake of our own greed, is a gross misappropriation of our God-given role as stewards of the planet.

One of the articles in the year-end issue of *U.S. News & World Report* several years ago was titled "10,000 Species to Disappear in 1991: Animals and Plants Vanishing Every Hour." It observed that twenty years ago, species were being silenced at a rate of about one a day; now, despite the efforts of conservationist and environmental groups, the rate is more than one per hour. "Within thirty years, mankind may have wiped out one fifth of all the earth's species."[8]

Why this incredible wholesale destruction of valuable life? The article continues with the observation that the causes of species extinction have changed in modern times. For centuries, human predation was a primary cause. People killed animals because their hides were beautiful or their flesh flavorful or because they competed with domestic animals for range land or attacked livestock. "Today, the killing is on a grander scale and far more impersonal, usually the result of development and resulting habitat loss."[9]

As Schaeffer suggests, the two factors that lead to the destruction of our environment are money and time—or to say it another way, greed and haste. It costs more money to treat the land well, be it for construction or safer environmental laws for industry or automobile manufacturing. It takes more time to treat the land properly, be it for reforestation, for personal recycling efforts, for energy saving by driving slower or walking or biking instead of driving. Both issues of money and time often center around greed, selfishness.

But the true Sabbath keeper refuses to allow time or money, haste or greed, to be the motivating factors for decisions relating to her or his job as God's tenant on this planet. The one who "plays heaven" with the planet is motivated by a respect for creation that comes from the recognition of the Creator. "If I love the Lover, I love what the Lover has made."

A simple thing like recycling personal garbage and waste could make a dent in the environmental waste problem. Shouldn't the Sabbath keeper be at the forefront of such attempts to manage life on this planet?

This is why the Sabbath is such an important theological concept. It provides us with a picture of God that motivates the believer to view the world from the proper perspective. It continually reminds us that God is a personal God who cares about His creation because He fashioned and made it with His own hands. He called it good. Then He gave to human beings the responsibility to manage it in His place, to be caretakers of the planet, stewards representing His interests in a world gone astray, co-workers in the Divine plan for global restoration. That theological perspective provided by the Sabbath shapes and molds our attitude and behavior toward all of life.

Bacchiocchi has rightly observed that it is only when people understand themselves and the world as the object of God's creation and redemption, that they will be both convinced and compelled to act as God's steward of their bodies as well as of the created order. "The Sabbath can play a vital role to help in recovering these spiritual values needed to solve the ecological crisis, since the day does provide the basis for both theological convictions and practical actions."[10]

For these reasons, the greatest hope of all for the world's environmental quagmire comes from people who are shaped and molded by such unyielding convictions, refusing to be intimidated or discouraged by the odds and risks. Like Barry and Janine Rands, in Mali, West Africa.[11] When the Rands arrived in the easternmost region of Mali, they took a good look around them. Too much tree cutting had contributed to unnatural disaster. Two major droughts and fifteen years of scant rain had turned the place into a wasteland. Trees that survived the drought were cut down for fuel and building material. The nomadic Tuareg people, once the aristocratic "lords of the desert," saw their whole way of life in jeopardy. Disease and suicide claimed many lives.

"We saw that if we were going to help, we had to address the ecological problems," Barry said.

So the Rands designed innovative projects that have helped reclaim the devastated environment. They focused on two things: using up less of the scarce wood supply and making the most of the rain that does fall on the desert.

Janine started by playing with mud. She kneaded clay, sand, and water until she found a mix that would stand intense heat. Then she designed a cookstove. The mud stove uses about half as much wood as the traditional three-rock fire, gives better heat, and is safer for children who play in cooking areas.

What's more, like any crucial test for a development project, the stoves have caught on by word of mouth. More than three thousand men and women have learned how to make them; more than seventeen thousand have been built.

Since the stoves need to be replaced periodically, the crafters have a steady source of extra income. Unlike many short-lived development projects, the mud stoves require absolutely nothing that is not locally and cheaply available.

Barry, meanwhile, concentrated on the water problem. He asked a group of former nomads who were interested in conservation: "If these ten glasses of water are all the rain that falls on our land this year, how many glasses soak into the ground for crops, trees, grass, and our wells, and how much runs off or evaporates?"

Some guessed half. Everyone underestimated the waste. Barry poured nine and a half glasses of water onto the ground. "That's how much we lose," he said.

"The high winds, hot climate, and hard rains we can't change. The trees and plants that used to catch water are gone. The good news is, we can do something to help the water soak in."

His audience learned to build rock and earth dikes along the contours of the land and to construct water catchments for planting trees. "In the Sahel," Barry explains, "the simpler things usually work best." The low contour dikes break the force of runoff water, so the silt stays behind the dikes instead of being carried off to some distant lake or swamp.

The people Barry spoke to that day went back to their homes and went to work. Before long they marveled at the results—green grass on a barren plain, soil wet enough after the first rain to plant trees and crops, and water already rising in the wells.

True, the amount of land that has been reclaimed is small. The desert is still growing. The Rands, however, measure achievement in the human spirit. "The people are realists," says Barry. "They understand that nothing's going to bring back the 'good old days.'"

"But they are realizing that they aren't helpless victims. They can fight back. They're prepared to adapt. That spirit of realistic optimism is the best thing that's happened so far."

What beautiful illustrations of the Sabbath keeper—God's people who go about their work as His tenants on this planet, persistently, regardless of the difficulties or odds, sometimes quietly, sometimes loudly, often without recognition or adulation, living their lives and doing what they do because it's right, trying their best to do what they think God would do, showing respect for all life.

2. An attitude of admiration. The second thing the Christian who "plays heaven" with the planet does is to nurture an attitude of admiration toward creation. It's learning to enjoy beauty and how it reveals God. It's an intentional attempt to develop an awareness of life that refuses to take things for granted. It's a deliberate contemplation of God's beauty in the earth for the sake of enjoyment and renewal of spirit.

In Thornton Wilder's play *Our Town,* Emily dies in childbirth but is granted a unique experience: the stage manager allows her to return from death and live one day of her life with her family. She has high hopes for that one day, but she ends up terribly disappointed. Just before she returns to her place in the cemetery, she reveals her frustration to the stage manager.

"We don't have time to look at one another." She breaks down, sobbing. "I didn't realize. So much that was going on and we never noticed. . . ."

Then she asks a profound question: "Do any human beings ever realize life while they live it—every, every minute?"

The stage manager replies, "No." Then after a pause, he says, "The saints and poets, maybe—they do some."[12]

Emily's observation challenges the Christian to live with awareness, realizing "life while we live it—every, every minute." The true Sabbath keeper, the one who "plays heaven" with the planet, develops such an appreciation of all that's going on around and inside, staying in touch with God through the creation, doing whatever it takes to pull the scales from the eyes that blind us from really seeing and appreciating God's presence in His creation. Thomas Merton, an American Trappist monk who was killed tragically by a freak electrocution while in Bangkok, Thailand, in 1968, wrote extensively on the importance of developing such an attitude toward life. He said:

> To be grateful is to recognize the love of God in everything He has given us—and He has given us everything. Every breath we draw is a gift of His love, every moment of existence is a grace, for it brings with it immense graces from Him. Gratitude takes nothing for granted, is never unresponsive, is constantly awakening to new wonder, and to praise of the goodness of God.[13]

This must be what the apostle Paul had in mind when he wrote, "Give thanks in all circumstances" (1 Thessalonians 5:18). Both he and Merton are talking about a way of living life, a particular perspective on and attitude about life—like Emily in the play who says, "realizing life while we live it," continually being aware of what's happening around us, developing the ability to see God and His presence everywhere. Admiration. Appreciation.

Vincent Van Gogh, the famous Dutch artist, wrote, "All nature seems to speak. . . . As for me, I cannot understand why everybody does not see it or feel it; nature or God does it for everyone who has eyes and ears and a heart to understand."[14]

Developing this attitude of admiration for creation, "grasping life at its depth," as Van Gogh wrote, is a challenge to our twentieth century lifestyles. Superficiality is encouraged. Everyone is so busy! There are so many urgent things to do, so many people to meet, so many books to read, so many events to attend. Either people's jobs demand time and overtime or they're unemployed and spend much of their time either looking for work or worrying about not finding it. Families need lots of time and energy. School studies could fill every waking hour. Houses, apartments, and yards beg for attention. People promise to do things for the church or community organizations.

There simply is not any time left—calendars are filled with appointments: doctors, dentists, music lessons, potlucks, meetings, and on and on. Hearts and minds only have time left for the big things, the big issues.

But true gratitude takes nothing for granted. It is aware of everything. It watches for opportunities to acknowledge God's presence, enabling a deep appreciation and admiration for God's creation to develop. That's why true gratitude is able to give thanks in everything.

Annie Dillard, in her Pulitzer Prize-winning book *Pilgrim at Tinker Creek,* does this in a most remarkable way. She takes the smallest, most mundane things of life and writes about them so vividly they practically come alive and jump off the page. In the book she makes the statement, "I cannot cause light; the most I can do is try to put myself in the path of its beam."[15] What she's saying is that the secret to really seeing life as God designed it is to intentionally place ourselves right smack-dab into the middle of life, with our eyes wide-open to everything around us. Only then will we experience the wonder of God's presence in His creation. Only then will we be able to nurture an appreciation and admiration for life—a spirit of gratitude and praise for everything.

This is where Sabbath keepers have a real advantage. The true Sabbath keeper is one who continually "plays heaven" with the planet. She/he responds to nature and this earth in two ways: first, by developing and nurturing an attitude of respect for all of life—seeing all life on this planet as fellow-creatures come from the same hand of God as ourselves and thus deserving our respect.

Second, the Sabbath keeper intentionally develops and nurtures an attitude of admiration for nature (for the sake of admiration). This is in opposition to an attitude that views nature as something to be used merely to accomplish some selfish goal—exploitation.

In *The Rebel,* Albert Camus wrote: "When nature ceases to be an object of contemplation and admiration, it can then be nothing more than material for an action that aims at transforming it."[16] In other words, when we lose the ability to view nature simply as life that can be admired for its beauty in its most natural state, we are led to exploit it for our own purposes, we use it and then abuse it.

Samuele Bacchiocchi agrees and concludes that the Sabbath is a day not to alter nature but to admire it as an expression of the beauty and glory of God's handiwork (Psalm 19:1). When was the last time you simply sat and watched a duck flying overhead or feeding in a pond or watched the golden leaves falling from the tree to the ground or watched the rain dripping from the roof and listened to its pitter-pat, just for the sake of enjoying it?

The temptation, instead, is to look at that duck as something to enjoy for sport or for cooking or to think of that falling leaf as fertilizer for our gardens or extra work to rake up or to see the rain and consider how to tap its energy or dam its resources. We get so busy in life, or become so pragmatic in living, that we develop an attitude of exploitation instead of admiration for nature—how to use nature and life for our own purposes rather than enjoying it simply as it is. Sabbath is God's gracious gift to help overcome that selfish tendency.

The Lord has been trying to teach me this vital lesson. It all began on a retreat I went to for one of my classes at Fuller Theological Seminary in Pasadena several years ago. We were at an old Benedictine monastery in the high desert above Los Angeles. We were supposed to take some time alone to read Scripture and write about it.

After breakfast one morning, I went outside to look around to see where I could go to do my meditation and journaling. This retreat center is in a beautiful, green oasis in the middle of the desert. But I have this obsession with climbing to the highest point around and not being satisfied until I am on top—it's for the sake of having a spectacular view, of course! I noticed the highest hill some distance from the retreat center, so I just had to go there even if it killed me.

I finally got to the top and sat there, out of breath, drinking in the incredible view. As I began to reflect about my life, my goals, my dreams, I came under the strong conviction that I was more concerned about what I could do in life than what I could be. I suddenly began to see that my preoccupation was with accomplishing things rather than becoming. I was so obsessed with trying to see and understand where God was in the bigger picture of my whole life that I was neglecting His presence in the smaller, seemingly insignificant things all around me. My obsession with climbing to the highest peaks in order to have an encounter with God was causing me to miss encountering Him in the valleys, forests, and the closed-in-areas of life.

The Lord was telling me in no uncertain terms that I needed intentionally to become more aware of looking for and sensing His presence everywhere I was—to learn to be satisfied with wherever I encountered Him, rather than always feeling that I had to go here or be there to really experience Him fully. Rather than always looking up to the high peaks, maybe I needed to look down and around more often, to live in the here and now rather than the future or past, to learn the art of admiration and appreciation of creation, big and small!

This was such a powerful conviction from the Lord that when I got ready to leave the retreat center, I went into their gift shop to look for something with which I could remember my special experience. Unbelievably, God had this plaque all ready for me. I had to buy it because the saying on it was exactly what He'd been trying to tell me. The plaque says, "There is no spot where God is not."

Little by little I'm learning the Sabbath keeper's art of taking nothing for granted—in everything giving thanks—an attitude of both respect and admiration for God's creation.

Notice how profoundly Annie Dillard does this as she writes

about watching something as simple, routine, and mundane as a tree reflecting the sun at sunset:

> One day I was walking along Tinker Creek thinking of nothing at all, and I saw the tree with the lights in it. I saw the backyard cedar, where the mourning doves roost, charged and transfigured, each cell buzzing with the flame. I stood on the grass with the lights in it, grass that was wholly fire, utterly focused and utterly dreamed. It was less like seeing than like being seen for the first time, knocked breathless by a powerful glance. The flood of fire abated, but I'm still spending the power.
>
> Gradually the lights went out in the cedar, the colors died, the cells unflamed and disappeared. I was still ringing. I had been my whole life a bell, and never knew it until at that moment I was lifted and struck. I have since only very rarely seen the tree with the light in it. The vision comes and goes, mostly goes, but I live for it, for the moment when the mountains open and a new light roars in spate through the crack, and the mountains slam.[17]

What a picturesque description of something as simple as a sunset! How is Annie Dillard able to view it with such depth? She has learned the Sabbath keeper's art of taking nothing for granted. She has developed an attitude of both respect and admiration for God's creation. By taking time to breathe deeply of life, she is able to connect with the Giver of life.

That sounds to me just like the psalmist in scripture. His imagination roamed the sea; he saw the sea's creatures, great and small, as God's playthings. He walked along the river, waded in the streams, sat quietly in the forest, and watched animals come to the water. His eyes and ears were really in love, discovering the world, penetrating beneath the surface and finding God. He realized life as he lived it, and for that reason he was able to celebrate life in gratitude, praise, and admiration.[18]

Isn't this what Paul had in mind when he said, "In everything give thanks?"

The Sabbath, pointing as it does to Creation and redemption/restoration, should place Sabbath keepers and the church in the forefront of those concerned for this planet. When the church genuinely begins to understand and experience the biblical meaning of the Sabbath, there will be a renewal of how it relates to the pressing human issues raising their ugly heads on this sin-stricken planet. Are you and I among those who "play heaven" with the family, the homeless, and the planet?

Chapter 14

Sabbath Worship and Church Revival

Gordon MacDonald tells about one of the famous eighteenth-century composers who had a rebellious son.[1] This boy gave his parents terrible heartaches. One of the things the boy enjoyed doing to make his father upset was this: coming in late at night after his father and mother had gone to bed, and before going to his own room, he would sit down at his dad's piano in the living room. Slowly, loudly, he'd play a simple scale, deliberately leaving out the final note. With the scale uncompleted, he would then retire to his room.

Meanwhile, his father, hearing the scale minus the final note, would toss and turn in his bed, going crazy, his mind unable to relax because the scale was unresolved. Finally, in consternation, he would groggily stumble down the stairs to his piano and hit the unstruck final note of the scale. Only then would his mind surrender to sleep once again.

That would drive me crazy too! We've all been created with the need for completion and resolution in our lives. So when we don't experience them, we feel frustrated, half ourselves—like there's a need for something more. Thousands of people live their lives in a search for that something more, never quite sure where to look, more often than not trying and experimenting in the wrong ways and places. But as one philosopher put it, "To have more does not mean to be more."[2]

So life gets faster and faster, the stakes go higher and higher, the cycle more and more vicious, the search more frantic until something finally has to give.

Back in the years of African colonial history, a traveler was making a long trek through the deep jungles. Coolies had been hired from a tribe to carry the loads of luggage. The first day's pace was fast and grueling. The group covered a lot of territory. The traveler had high hopes of a speedy journey. But on the second morning these jungle tribesmen refused to move.

The traveler spoke with authority: "Get up! We must go, now!"

They just sat there and wouldn't budge. He shouted, he threatened, he bribed, he even pleaded—no results. They just sat there motionless. Finally, in exasperation he asked them why they were behaving so strangely.

The spokesman replied, "Bwana, we go too fast the first day. Now we wait for our souls to catch up with our bodies."

These jungle tribesmen recognized a significant aspect to experiencing that sense of completeness and resolution in our lives—our pace of life is so fast that unless we have regular times in which we stop everything and refocus, let our souls catch up with our bodies, so to speak, we remain unresolved and incomplete.

This is why times for worship and praise to God are so vital for the building and restoring of the spiritual life. The Sabbath is God's gracious gift to us, providing the opportunity every week to come together as a community of faith for this time of refocusing, renewing, and resolving. And when the content of our refocusing becomes praise to God for His Goodness, things really begin to happen.

There's a lot of talk in the Seventh-day Adventist Church right now about revival and reformation and the outpouring of the Holy Spirit. Our world church leaders and many others have been writing profusely in all the major Seventh-day Adventist magazines about this, calling the church to a spiritual renewal.

Yet absent in much of this discussion has been an emphasis on the importance of renewal in corporate worship and how it relates to revival and reformation. Instead, Adventist conversations about worship often degenerate into heated debates about worship styles, what's right and what's wrong? Should music be contemporary or traditional, should singing be accompanied by an organ and piano or a band of guitars, synthesizers, and drums? Should multimedia be in worship? What about drama? What about words to the songs—is it better to read them off of a screen or a hymnal?

We've become so polarized on this issue of worship that we've lost sight of the whole purpose of worship. We've become so focused on the methodology that we've blurred the theology. Consequently, discussion about revival, renewal, and reformation in the church often excludes worship renewal—it's too controversial a topic.

But is it possible for genuine revival and reformation to take place in isolation from corporate worship renewal? And what should corporate worship renewal involve?

Hezekiah's experience recorded in 2 Chronicles 29-31 provides incredible evidence that, when there is a renewal of worship and praise individually and corporately, real revival and reformation will come. Notice how this process takes place.

Hezekiah was raised during one of the lowest periods of Judah's history, with his father, King Ahaz, leading the people into spiritual apostasy and rebellion against God. Imagine this young boy, at some point in his early life, watching as his father takes one of his own brothers and, in the name of God, lays him on the altar, steps back, and stands there watching as his son burns to death. What an impression that must have made on Hezekiah! Perhaps then and there, this boy vowed that if he became king someday, he would do things differently!

At twenty-five years of age, Hezekiah became king. Now it was all up to him. It didn't take him long to figure out what he wanted to do. He'd been thinking about this for years, just waiting for the opportunity. He had devised a three-part plan.

Part one: Open up the church again for worship. In the first month of his reign as king, Hezekiah walked up the steps to the great temple door in Jerusalem, the door that his father had shut in recognition of the victory of Assyria's gods. With the help of his soldiers and priests, he broke the beams keeping the doors closed, and with a shout of victory, threw open those huge doors. The temple was open again!

Word spread like wildfire. "The king has opened the temple doors! The king has opened the temple doors! We're free from the domination of Assyria's power. We're free—independent!" Everyone waits in anticipation for what will happen next.

Part two: Revitalize the worship leaders. Hezekiah's plan next involves the spiritual leaders of the nation, the priests and Levites. Calling them all together to the east side of the temple, he addresses them:

" 'Listen to me, Levites! Consecrate yourselves now and consecrate the temple of the LORD, the God of your fathers. Remove all defilement from the sanctuary. Our fathers were unfaithful; they did evil in the eyes of the LORD our God and forsook him. They turned their faces away from the LORD's dwelling place and turned their backs on him. They also shut the doors of the portico and put out the lamps. They did not burn incense or present any burnt offerings at the sanctuary to the God of Israel. Therefore, the anger of the LORD has fallen on Judah and Jerusalem; he has made them an object of dread and horror and scorn, as you can see with your own eyes. This is why our fathers have fallen by the sword and why our sons and daughters and our wives are in captivity. Now I intend to make a covenant with the LORD, the God of Israel, so that his fierce anger will turn away from us. My sons, do not be negligent now, for the LORD has chosen you to stand before him and serve him, to minister before him and to burn incense' " (2 Chron. 29:5-11).

As the leader of the kingdom, Hezekiah calls first for the spiritual renewal of his leaders, the spiritual directors of the people. How can there be revival and reformation among the people unless God's leaders are renewed themselves?

So the priests and Levites assemble themselves together and begin consecration. Numbers 19 describes the following process of purification:

A red heifer without defect or blemish is killed. The high priest takes some of its blood on his finger and sprinkles it seven times toward the front of the temple. The body of the heifer is burned. The priest takes some cedar wood, hyssop, and scarlet wool and throws them onto the burning heifer. Then the ashes are gathered up and placed in the basin of water, the water of cleansing and purification.

One by one, the priests and Levites come forward to wash themselves with this water of cleansing, symbolizing a purification from sins by the Savior's blood.

Then, once cleaned, consecrated, and purified, the men go into the temple to do the same. They begin bringing out into the courtyard all the unclean things from the temple, put there by Ahaz and his leaders. They take these idolatrous items down to the Kidron Valley—the very spot where King Ahaz sacrificed his sons—to be burned.

For sixteen days this work of consecration goes on. Finally it is done. Hezekiah gathers the priests, Levites, and city officials together. Now it's time for worship and praise.

The first part of their worship involves a confession of and atonement for their sins. As they watch the sacrifices burn, they realize that death must take place because of sin—their sins. But because of the willing sacrifice of God, their separation from Him is over. His love and grace bridge the gap. Through Him, reconciliation is complete.

No wonder this is followed by rapturous songs of praise. Hezekiah has stationed the Levites in the temple with cymbals, harps, and guitars (lyres). The priests are there with their trumpets. The singers are ready and waiting.

The king gives the signal. As another burnt offering is placed upon the altar, the music breaks out. The whole assembly joins in and then bows in worship. God is good, God is gracious, God is merciful and faithful! Praise His name!

From this context of praise, Hezekiah now invites the spiritual leaders to bring offerings of thanksgiving to God. So the whole assembly returns with sacrifices and thank offerings. What a scene of praise and joy. In fact, the story says they sing songs of praise with gladness (2 Chron. 29:30). All the people rejoice at what God has brought about for His people so quickly. God is good!

But that's not the end of their renewal. Part three of Hezekiah's plan for worship renewal: *Revitalize the people of God, the congregation.* So far, the activities have been primarily for the spiritual leaders of the nation. Now Hezekiah sends word out to all the people of the nation, even including their brothers and sisters from Israel, to come for a big celebration of the Passover. He calls for the people to join in spiritual renewal.

Many are surprised and excited. The Passover hasn't been celebrated for years and years, especially with all of God's people, both Israel and Judah. This is a new day! As the couriers go from town to town, giving the king's call, they meet with mixed reactions. Some scorn and ridicule them. This is the last thing they're interested in doing. After all, this kind of large scale activity is sure to arouse the anger of Assyria. It will be viewed as a movement for independence.

Many are afraid to come. But hundreds and thousands of others are thrilled to death. At last, a celebration in Jerusalem, at the temple of God! They wouldn't miss this for the world.

They come from everywhere and gather in Jerusalem at the great temple. The sense of anticipation and expectancy is high. Finally the signal is given, the rams' horns are blown, and the celebration begins. The Passover lambs are killed, the blood is sprinkled on the people and the temple, and then portions of the meat are given to the people to eat.

Families sit together. The story of the great Exodus, God's gracious deliverance of their forefathers from slavery and bondage in Egypt, is told and retold—how on that awesome night, the angel of death passed over those homes that had confessed their sins and shown their faith in God's grace and love by sprinkling blood from the lamb on their doorposts.

So as parents and children eat the lamb, they confess their sins to each other and to God. With every bite, they remember that it is God's grace and mercy that save them when their sins should bring them death instead.

Real worship always involves a confession of sins to God, a recognition that God is the One who saves, not we. That is a significant element in worship renewal. In the words of the great theologian James Denny, "No man can bear witness to Christ and to himself at the same time. No man can give the impression that he is clever and that Christ is mighty to save."

That's why another author wrote, "The greatest act of faith is when a man decides that he is not God."[3] Confession of who God is and who we are accomplish that.

While this is going on, the Levites and priests, with all their instruments, play and sing songs of praise to God. It's an incredibly festive and joyous celebration of worship. For seven days, the people celebrate God. In fact, there's so much praise and joy that when the seven days are over, they all vote to stay seven more days (30:23).

The effect of this worship renewal on the people, as the story says, is that there is incredible joy in Jerusalem. "Since the days of Solomon son of David king of Israel there had been nothing like this in Jerusalem" (30:26).

A renewal of worship and praise always has that kind of an effect on people. It brings joy and peace into our lives to spend time acknowledging God and His great love and goodness, to spend time praising Him, singing to Him, confessing ourselves to Him. It rejuvenates us, letting our souls catch up with our bodies. Only worship and praise of God bring our unresolved lives to resolution, our sense of incompleteness to completeness, our fragmentation to wholeness.

This is why the Sabbath is such an incredibly gracious gift from God that we would do well to experience more fully and regularly. It provides that significant opportunity for corporate praise and worship. Entering into the Sabbath experience every week teaches the church how to praise and worship more deeply as God's people.

Abraham Heschel acknowledges this aspect of the Sabbath when he writes:

> It is the Sabbath that inspires all the creatures to sing praise to the Lord. In the language of the Sabbath morning liturgy:
> "To God who rested from all action on the seventh day and ascended upon His throne of glory.
> He vested the day of rest with beauty;
> He called the Sabbath a delight.
> This is the song and the praise of the seventh day, on which God rested from His work.
> The seventh day itself is uttering praise.
> A song of the Sabbath day:
> 'It is good to give thanks unto the Lord!'
> Therefore, all creatures of God bless Him.
> The Sabbath teaches all beings whom to praise.[4]

But that's not all Sabbath worship renewal does. Look at what happens next. The story is found in 2 Chronicles 31. When the people leave the temple to return home, they go all over the land in both Judah and Israel, smashing the sacred stones and idols, cutting down the Asherah poles, destroying the high places and altars. They have rejected idolatry and all it stands for.

They're finally acknowledging that Yahweh, the God of their forefathers, is their God. In this incredibly bold act, they are essentially telling the great power of Assyria, "We no longer trust in your power for our needs. We're no longer going to rely on human power. We're committing ourselves to trusting in God! He is most important now!"

This is what worship and praise do for us. They help us regain focus and perspective about what's really important in life.

"God is of no importance unless He is of supreme importance."[5]

The worshipping people in this story are brought to that realization and commitment.

Genuine worship and praise lead us to own the prayer of Dag Hammarskjold, who said, "For all that has been, thanks. For all that shall be, yes."[6] Whatever God wants us to do, we are willing.

But the smashing of idols isn't the only evidence of revival and reformation these people exhibit from their worship and praise experience. When King Hezekiah gives his tithes and offerings to the temple and then calls the people to do the same, they respond so generously that additional storehouses have to be built in the temple to keep the overflow. The result is that God is praised and the people are blessed.

This is the way it works. When you really experience God, you want to live generously. Brennan Manning makes the statement: "The more rooted we are in the love of God, the more generously we live our faith and practice it."[7]

Then this generosity begins to overflow in the way we treat other people.

This experience of Hezekiah and the people shows that when there is a renewal of worship and praise, with the content being a celebration of God's grace, goodness, and activity in our lives, using the elements of confession, songs of praise, and gifts of thanksgiving, then real revival and reformation will come. It will manifest itself by our priorities and our values. We will place supreme importance on knowing God, trusting Him implicitly, and living generously for others. It all stems first from worship and praise.

Robert Webber, in his book *Worship Is a Verb,* makes this statement:

> Evangelism is an exceedingly important work of the church, as is teaching, fellowship, servanthood, missions, and the healing of broken lives. But it is worship that really stands behind all these activities. The church is first a worshipping community. Evangelism and other functions of ministry flow from the worship of the church.[8]

No wonder God graciously reminds us not only in the heart of His law but elsewhere in Scripture to remember the Sabbath day to keep it holy. Our lives desperately need this weekly time for corporate worship and praise, a time in which we come together to acknowledge the supremacy of God in our lives and our solidarity with the human family as God's children.

Personal, individual worship and devotional times are vital in the growing spiritual life. But as this story of Hezekiah and his people shows, if there is to be genuine church renewal, revival, and reformation, there must be a revitalization of corporate worship as well.

Chapter 15

The Purpose of Corporate Sabbath Worship

For this revitalization of corporate Sabbath worship to take place, there must be a renewed emphasis within the worship itself on the following:

1. Worship celebrates God's activity in our lives. We are in grave danger, both within and without the church, of becoming so caught up in the rounds of our busy activities that we lose sight of God and His activity in our lives. So our tendency, when we come to worship, is to celebrate our work instead of His. We focus on our commitment to Him rather than on His commitment to us.

Eugene Peterson puts us back on target when he insightfully observes that not too many of us preach vigorously on the seventh commandment and then go on to pursue lives of active adultery. In the same way, not many of us preach eloquently on the second commandment and then moonlight by selling plastic fertility goddesses in the narthex. "But we conscientiously catechize our people on the fourth commandment and without a blush flaunt our workaholic Sabbath-breaking as evidence of an extraordinary piety."

And then he goes on to suggest the following definitions of Sabbath and Sabbath keeping:

> Sabbath: uncluttered time and space to distance ourselves from the frenzy of our own activities so we can see what God has been and is doing. If we do not regularly quit work for one day a week we take ourselves far too seriously. The moral sweat pouring off our brows blinds us to the primal action of God in and around us.
>
> Sabbath-keeping: Quieting the internal noise so we hear the still small voice of our Lord. Removing the distractions of pride so we discern the presence of Christ. [1]

Unless corporate Sabbath worship has as its focus God's activity, we remain blinded by our own preoccupations and pride. We desperately need to see God and His power.

How can this be accomplished? In two ways: first, in a spirit of festivity and celebration. Robert Webber has pointed out that psychiatrists recognize the need for festivity as a release from the pressures of work and ambition. They insist that festivity puts us in touch with another realm of life—with the fanciful and the imaginative. It puts us in contact with a sense of the supernatural, the otherworldly, the mystery of life. God built into each of us the capability to dream, tell stories, act, and communicate with Him and each other through festivity.

The significant implication of this, as Webber goes on to suggest, is that worship taps into this side of our personality. It affirms it, releases it, and frees us to experience Christ through the festive occasion that celebrates Him.

In this way, "celebrative worship contradicts the secular reduction of the human person into a mere economic, intellectual, or technological entity. . . . Consequently, worship lifts the worshiper out of drudgery and brings meaning to life."[2]

And second, coming to worship in this spirit of festivity and celebration of God and His power enables us to worship in a spirit of trust—to recognize that through good and bad times, God is still active.

When the congregation sings God's praises, reads and hears God's Word, gives to Him and receives from Him, the focus is completely on God's power and faithfulness. For those worshipers who are experiencing discouragement and disillusionment from various life situations, pain from loss or uncertainty, this focus on God enables them to worship in a spirit of trust that though God doesn't appear active in their lives at the present, because He is a faithful God, He will act on their behalf.

2. Worship recenters, refocuses, regains perspective by stopping to pay attention to the signposts. Corporate Sabbath worship, if it's going to be renewing, must spend time answering the question, "What are the signposts along the road of our lives that point to God's presence?" Spending time recognizing those evidences of God helps to put our lives back into perspective.

This activity in worship can be called "paradigm shifting." Why is this so vital to the church's revitalization and renewal? Stephen Covey, in his book *The Seven Habits of Highly Effective People,* discusses the significance of paradigms. He observes that our paradigms, correct or incorrect, are the sources of our attitudes and behaviors, and ultimately our relationships with others.

So if we want to make significant change, we need to work on our basic paradigms. Paradigms are powerful because they create the lens through which we see the world. "The power of a paradigm shift is the essential power of quantum change, whether that shift is an instantaneous or a slow and deliberate process."[3]

Covey tells the following personal story to illustrate the nature and power of a paradigm shift. He was riding on the subway in New York City one Sunday morning. People were sitting quietly—some reading newspapers, some lost in thought, some resting with their eyes closed. It was a calm, peaceful scene.

Then suddenly, a man and his children entered the subway car. The children were so loud and rambunctious that instantly the whole climate changed.

The man sat down next to him and closed his eyes, apparently oblivious to the situation. The children were yelling back and forth, throwing things, even grabbing people's papers. It was very disturbing! Yet, the man sitting next to him did nothing about it.

It was difficult not to feel irritated. Covey couldn't believe that the man could be so insensitive as to let his children run wild like that and do nothing about it, taking no responsibility at all. It was easy to see that everyone else on the subway felt irritated too.

So finally, with what Covey felt was unusual patience and restraint, he turned to the man and said, "Sir, your children are really disturbing a lot of people. I wonder if you couldn't control them a little more?"

The man lifted his gaze as if to come to a consciousness of the situation for the first time and said softly, "Oh, you're right. I guess I should do something about it. We just came from the hospital where their mother died about an hour ago. I don't know what to think, and I guess they don't know how to handle it either."

Can you imagine what Covey felt at that moment? His paradigm shifted. Suddenly he saw things differently, and because he saw differently, he thought differently, he felt differently, he behaved differently.

Here's how he described it:

> My irritation vanished. I didn't have to worry about controlling my attitude or my behavior; my heart was filled with the man's pain. Feelings of sympathy and compassion flowed freely. "Your wife just died? Oh, I'm so sorry! Can you tell me about it? What can I do to help?" Everything changed in an instant.[4]

Corporate Sabbath worship, for it to accomplish the renewal God wants it to for us, must utilize paradigm shifting—deliberate and intentional refocusing and recentering. That is the spiritual dynamic God gives to us to experience lasting change.

"And we, who with unveiled faces all reflect the Lord's glory, are being transformed into his likeness with ever-increasing glory" (2 Corinthians 3:18).

"Do not conform any longer to the pattern of this world, but be transformed by the renewing of your mind" (Romans 12:2).

"As [a man] thinks in his heart, so is he" (Proverbs 23:7, NKJV).

Who is most important? The vital paradigm shifts that corporate Sabbath worship must provide are, first, the truth that life revolves around God, not me. It must answer the questions, Who and what is most important in life?

Webber writes again:

> We don't go to worship to celebrate what we have done. We don't say, "Look, Lord, isn't it wonderful that I believe in you, follow you, and serve you!" No! We go to worship to praise and thank God for what He has done, is doing, and will do. God's work in Christ is the focus of worship. And it is the focus we need to recapture as we seek to renew our public worship experience.[5]

So why is this focus so important? Webber goes on to observe that we live in a world where the gods of contemporary civilization grab for our attention and commitment. The gods of materialism, pleasure, sensualism, and success at any cost, which plague us on a daily basis, need to be exposed for what they are. In beholding our God, these gods that would divert us and send us away from Christ are exposed and sent on the run.

So worship is not complete without beholding our God, without seeing and experiencing the greatness of His power and love. "Then, once we have beheld God, we are in a position to listen to Him. . . . When we behold Him, He prepares us to listen to His voice, to direct our paths, to lead us into His loving will for our lives."[6]

Why are we important? The second paradigm shift that corporate Sabbath worship must provide is the natural extension of the first one—once it is clear who is most important, namely God, then we are prepared to recognize what makes us important.

Contrary to the perspective we're so easily seduced into believing during the busy work week, in Sabbath worship we're reminded that work does not tell us our worth. It's not what we do but who we are as God's children that gives us value and worth, that really matters.

Once again Webber observes:

> Secularism has also affected worship through its distorted understanding of human personality. Since secularism lacks a supernatural view of the person, it seeks to define personhood apart from the biblical concept that we are created in the image of God. Instead, to the secularists, persons are defined in terms of economics, thought, or production. Karl Marx defined a person in terms of work: what do you do? The philosopher Descartes defined a person in terms of mind: what do you think? And the technological revolution defined a person through production: what have you done? Worship that is principally geared toward dispensing intellectual information or pressing for results—massive church memberships or decisions—has already capitulated to the secular attitude. It reduces human personality to a brain or a product, and worship deteriorates into nothing more than information for the mind or a product for the producer.[7]

For this reason, promotion must be kept to a bare minimum during Sabbath corporate worship (during the announcement time as well as the offering appeal). It's so easy to fall into the trap of using the church service to promote programs or needs in the church that we want people to be involved in. After all, church is the one time when the most amount of people are gathered together, right? But consequently, the service degenerates into a promotional hour rather than real worship of God. A life-changing paradigm-shift cannot take place.

Gayland Richardson has written a beautiful Sabbath morning prayer that poignantly puts in perspective this need:

> O God, all week we have heard that soap makes us clean, wealth makes us happy, youth makes us desirable, and fame gives us purpose. Forgive us for believing these things to be true.
>
> This morning teach us that Your grace makes us clean; that happiness comes from the contentment of seeing life from Your viewpoint. Teach us that we are valuable, important, and desirable because we are Your children. And may our purpose be found in the pleasure of Your presence. Amen.[8]

So corporate Sabbath worship must give us a twofold paradigm shift: God is the most important One in life, and we are important, not for what we do but because He has made us His children (who we are).

Marva Dawn resoundingly reiterates this good news when, in commenting on the first four verses of Isaiah 43, she notes that within the context of God's promises to rescue his people from their captivity and bring the exiles back to their home, this passage focuses on God's overt declaration of what makes his people worthy. Over and over the text insists, as she points out, that Yahweh is the One who makes us valuable. He is the One who created, formed, redeemed, called His people by name, made them His, was with them, protected them, saved them, and made them precious and honored in His sight.

As she goes on to observe, God certainly didn't choose Israel because of their accomplishments or their productivity. They were the least among the people of the ancient Near East. They were rebellious and self-centered. They constantly failed to keep their end of the covenant relationship with Yahweh. So God's love for them is obviously not related to what they do but to His character as the eternal I AM.

"This is what we celebrate on the Sabbath day," Dawn concludes. "We join the generations of believers—going all the way back to God's people, the Israelites—who set aside a day to remember that we are precious and honored in God's sight and loved, profoundly loved, not because of what we produce."[9]

This must be the focus in our corporate worship experience if the church is going to enjoy revitalization, renewal, revival, and reformation. Only when the people experience God's graciousness and goodness will they be enabled to live out their faith generously. That's what Hezekiah's story shows too. Through this regular encounter with the love of God, the grace of Jesus Christ, and the fellowship of the Holy Spirit, in the company of the family of believers, we will receive security, confidence, and boldness to live for Him moment by moment, regardless of the circumstances or the costs.

In *Loving God,* Charles Colson tells the story of a Russian Jew named Boris Nicholayevich Kornfeld.[10] As a medical doctor, Kornfeld found himself in the gulag for reasons that weren't very clear to him. But because of his medical training, he became a rather important person in the prison. He didn't receive any special privileges, but he was able to care for the sick.

One of his jobs he particularly hated. It was to sign medical release forms for men who were to be punished in the box. The box was a tiny cubicle in which men would be forced to crouch for days on end, in the Siberian winter, living in their own excrement, eating the meagerest of rations. The medical release certified that the victim was physically able to withstand the ordeal. It was essentially a death warrant. Kornfeld hated doing this, but so did all the other doctors in the gulag. What could he do, anyway?

In the course of his duties, Kornfeld met a Christian who told him of Jesus, his Messiah. What most captured Kornfeld's attention was the way this Messiah died. Like Kornfeld, Jesus had been arrested and imprisoned without just cause. Soon Kornfeld was converted. He'd never known such joy and peace! Now he was a prisoner on the outside but free on the inside.

With his newfound faith, things began to change for Kornfeld, the first being that he would no longer sign the hated medical release forms. This infuriated the authorities, but they needed his medical expertise, so they let it slide.

Now that Kornfeld was looking at the world through different eyes, other things had to change too. The prison had its "trustees," ruthless men who were prisoners themselves but who served the prison authorities in exchange for certain privileges. These traitors would wander the halls of the prison hospital, stuffing their mouths with the white bread set there on trays for men suffering from pellagra. White bread was all these men's stomachs could digest, and the trustees were taking it from them to stuff themselves. Although it was officially illegal, no one ever said anything about it for fear of revenge. But Kornfeld was a new man in Christ, and now he would speak!

One day he saw a trustee stealing the bread for the pellagra patients, and he reported him to the authorities. The authorities couldn't have cared less, but to save face they were forced to punish the guilty man by putting him in the box for a few days.

The authorities were amazed by what this irritating Kornfeld had forced them to do, but they took comfort in the fact that undoubtedly he would be murdered when the trustee got out of the box. Kornfeld was as good as dead. He knew it, and so did everyone else.

One of Kornfeld's patients was a young man recovering from cancer surgery. Although heavily sedated with morphine, the patient, drifting in and out of consciousness, would catch bits and phrases from Dr. Kornfeld about his faith in Christ. Kornfeld wasn't really sure the man could hear him, but he faithfully worshipped and witnessed to God's love every day.

One night, after Kornfeld had been talking to this patient about God again and had just left his room, the patient heard a commotion outside. It had happened; Kornfeld had been murdered, clubbed to death by eight mallet blows to the head.

End of story? Not quite. On the strength of Kornfeld's witness, the cancer patient became a Christian. His name? Alexander Solzhenitszyn! As a result, one of the most famous Russians in the world today is not a Communist but a Christian!

When we really experience God in all His goodness, which is what worship and praise help us to do, we will be enabled to live for Him moment by moment, regardless of the circumstances or the costs. "The more rooted we are in the love of God," which happens from our worship and praise of Him, "the more generously we live our faith and practice it," which is what true revival and reformation are all about.

Conclusion

A group of researchers studying the effects of stress several years ago used twin lambs as subjects of an interesting experiment. For the first part of their experiment, one of the lambs was placed in a pen all alone. Electrical pulsing devices were hooked up at several feeding locations in the pen. As the lamb wandered to each feeding station in the enclosure, the researchers gave the lamb a short burst of electrical current. Each time this happened, the lamb would twitch and scamper to another part of the pen. The lamb never returned to the same location once it had been shocked.

This was repeated at each feeding station until the frightened lamb stood in the center of the pen shaking. He had no place to run. There were shocks everywhere. Completely overcome and filled with anxiety and stress, the lamb had a nervous breakdown.

The second part of the experiment involved the first lamb's twin brother. The researchers took him and put him in the same pen. Only this time they put his mother in the pen with him. Presently, they shocked him at the feeding station. Like his twin brother, he immediately twitched and ran—only he ran directly to his mother. He snuggled closely to her while she grunted softly in his ear.

She apparently reassured him because the lamb promptly returned to the exact spot where he was shocked the first time. The researchers threw the switch again. Again the lamb ran to his mother. Again she grunted in his ear, and again he returned to the same place.

This happened over and over, but as long as there was a reference point for the lamb to return to after each shock, he could handle the stress. He was able to cope.

The Sabbath is just such a reference point. Amidst the shocks and traumas of daily living, there's a palace in time that descends from heaven to earth each seventh day where we can find comfort and reassurance. Retreating to the palace of the King, we can receive strength to face the tensions and traumas of life. There in the arms of God, the Divine Romancer, we become emboldened to go out and live life with absolute confidence.

Certainly Rabbi Heschel had this reference point in mind when he wrote:

> In the tempestuous ocean of time and toil there are islands of stillness where man may enter a harbor and reclaim his dignity. The island is the seventh day, the Sabbath, a day of detachment from things, instruments and practical affairs as well as of attachment to the spirit. . . . The seventh day is the exodus from tension, the liberation of man from his own muddiness, the installation of man as a sovereign in the world of time.[1]

One of the critical new trends that George Barna describes in his book *The Frog in the Kettle* that's shaping and will continue to shape our society in the third millennium is the new concept of time. For several thousand years, people have used money as the primary means of establishing value. But Barna believes that by

2000 we will have shifted to using time as our dominant indicator of value.

It's the one resource that cannot be manufactured. It's a nonrenewable resource that limits our ability to experience all that we can. Every day we feel the frustration of not having enough time to do all the things we want. So, Barna predicted, "in the '90s and beyond, more and more of us will pay to protect our time. That is, money will be used to guard the more valuable commodity, time."[2]

What will be the result? People will look for businesses that save them time and make their lives more convenient. They'll focus on products and services that allow them the greatest flexibility with their time and the highest productivity for each minute.

As Barna goes on to describe, during this generation society will begin to focus on a new concept of success—success will not be viewed as having as much to do with acquisition as with control. In other words, the person who can put the pieces of his/her hectic, fast-paced, fragmented, out-of-control life together in such a way as to make sense out of this fast-paced, nonconventional way of life will be seen as successful. The person who can master time will define success.

So people will be looking for ways to help them take control of their time and of their hectic lives. It would seem, then, how much more valuable God's gift of His Sabbath should become in these days, months, and years ahead. The Sabbath is an oasis in time that cannot be controlled or manipulated or taken away by anyone else. How much both the church and society need the Sabbath.

No wonder even that great United States president, Abraham Lincoln, once said, "As we keep or break the Sabbath day, we nobly save or meanly lose the last and best hope by which man arises."[3] Little did he know how prophetic his words would be over a century and a half later.

The great needs in our society, matched by the great gift of the Sabbath from God, are what inspired Dr. Ernest R. Palen, a minister of the Reformed Church of America, in a sermon preached on March 13, 1966, in New York City, to emphasize:

> Our madly rushing, neurotic society needs the therapy of silence and quietness that flows from a day kept holy, really holy. A day when our thoughts are of God, our actions are tempered by a desire to serve God and our families, a day that is so different from the other days that it could make us different in our relationships to God and to our fellow man.[4]

How can we neglect such a gracious gift from God? Can we afford to let this gift sit on the shelf of our spiritual, theological, and religious libraries collecting dust? The renewal and revitalization of the church is at stake. How we in this generation choose to respond will affect not only our lives but the health and welfare of future generations. God help us to choose today to enter more fully into His glorious and gracious Sabbath rest.

Endnotes

CHAPTER 1

1. Charles Colson, *Presenting Belief in an Age of Unbelief* (Wheaton, Ill.: Victor Books, 1986), 5, 6.

2. Quoted in James Reichley, *Religion in American Public Life* (Washington, D.C.: Brookings Institution, 1985), 360.

3. Statistics drawn from Gallup Poll 1985, quoted by Donald C. Posterski, *Reinventing Evangelism: New Strategies for Presenting Christ in Today's World* (Downers Grove, Ill.: InterVarsity Press, 1989), 62.

4. Dean Borgman, "Faculty Letter to Our Alumni," quoted by Posterski, Gordon Conwell Seminary, May 1988, 21.

5. The statistics in the following paragraphs are taken from Peter L. Benson and Michael J. Donahue, "Valuegenesis: Report 2" (Minneapolis, Minn.: Search Institute, for the NAD Office of Education of S.D.A., Silver Spring, Md., February 15, 1991).

6. Posterski, 55, 56.

7. George Barna, *The Frog in the Kettle: What Christians Need to Know About Life in the Year 2000* (Ventura, Calif.: Regal Books, 1990), 26, 27.

8. Frederick Buechner, *The Magnificent Defeat* (New York: Seabury,

1979), 65.

9. Quoted in Philip Yancey, *Disappointment With God* (Grand Rapids, Mich.: Zondervan Publishing House, 1988), 253.

CHAPTER 2

1. A. E. Millgram, *The Sabbath: The Day of Delight* (Philadelphia: The Jewish Publication Society of America, 1947), 187.

2. *Webster's Collegiate Dictionary,* fifth edition (Springfield, Mass.: G. & C. Merriam Co., 1936), 1055.

3. "The Sabbath," *The Pulpit* 2 (February, 1917), XII:40.

4. M. L. Andreason, *The Sabbath* (Hagerstown, Md.: Review and Herald Publishing Association, 1969), 28.

5. Ibid., 30, 31.

6. *A Love Song for the Sabbath* (Hagerstown, Md.: Review and Herald Publishing Association, 1988), 68.

7. Ibid.

8. Oswald Chambers, *My Utmost for His Highest* (New York: Dodd, Mead and Co., 1954), 297.

9. Andreason, 28.

10. Harold H. P. Dressler, "The Sabbath in the Old Testament," *From Sabbath to LORD's Day: A Biblical, Historical, and Theological Investigation,* ed. D. A. Carson (Grand Rapids, Mich.: Zondervan Publishing House, 1982), 32.

11. Gerhard F. Hasel, and W. G. C. Murdoch, "The Sabbath in the Prophetic and Historical Literature of the Old Testament," *The Sabbath in Scripture and History,* ed. Kenneth A. Strand (Hagerstown, Md.: Review and Herald Publishing Association, 1982), 36; ibid., 50.

12. All scripture quotations, unless otherwise stated, are from The Holy Bible, New International Version (New York: International Bible Society, 1978).

13. Quoted by Herbert E. Saunders, *The Sabbath: Symbol of Creation and Re-Creation* (Plainfield, N.J.: American Sabbath Tract Society, 1970), 22.

14. Ellen G. White, *The Great Controversy Between Christ and Satan* (Nampa, Idaho: Pacific Press® Publishing Association, 1950), 438.

15. George Elliot, *The Abiding Sabbath,* 1884, pages 17, 18; quoted

by Samuele Bacchiocchi in *Divine Rest for Human Restlessness* (Rome: The Pontifical Gregorian University Press, 1980), 70.

16. Mordecai M. Kaplan, "Affiliation With the Synagogue," *The Jewish Communal Register* (New York: 1917), 118, 119; also quoted in A. E. Millgram, p. 7.

CHAPTER 3

1. Quoted by Eugene H. Peterson in "The Unselfing of America," *Christianity Today* (5 April 1985): 31.

2. Eugene H. Peterson, *Working the Angles: The Shape of Pastoral Integrity* (Grand Rapids, Mich.: Eerdmans Publishing Co., 1987), 45.

3. Brennan Manning, *Lion and Lamb: The Relentless Tenderness of Jesus* (Old Tappan, N.J.: Chosen Books, 1986), 163.

4. Ibid., 160.

5. *Time* (6 August 1990): 61, 62.

6. Gordon MacDonald, *Ordering Your Private World* (Nashville, Tenn.: Thomas Nelson Publishers, 1984), 164.

7. Gordon MacDonald, *Restoring Your Spiritual Passion* (Nashville, Tenn.: Thomas Nelson Publishers, 1986), 157, 158.

8. Marva J. Dawn, *Keeping the Sabbath Wholly: Ceasing, Resting, Embracing, Feasting* (Grand Rapids, Mich.: Eerdmans Publishing Co., 1989), 50.

9. Viktor E. Frankl, *Man's Search for Meaning,* third edition (New York: Simon and Schuster, 1984), 82-84.

10. Bacchiocchi, 57.

CHAPTER 4

1. Garth Lean, *God's Politician* (London: Darton, Longman & Todd, 1980), 89; quoted by Gordon MacDonald, *Ordering Your Private World,* 161-163.

2. Ibid., 163.

3. Quoted in Bacchiocchi, 94.

4. *Parables, Etc.,* vol. 10, no. 6 (August 1990): 6.

5. MacDonald, 164.

CHAPTER 5

1. Bacchiocchi, 66, 67.

2. Ibid., 67.

3. Sakae Kubo, *God Meets Man: A Theology of the Sabbath and Second Advent* (Nashville, Tenn.: Southern Publishing Association, 1978), 39, 43.

4. Karl Barth, *Church Dogmatics, III.4*, 56, 57, quoted in Paul K. Jewett, *The Lord's Day: A Theological Guide to the Christian Day of Worship* (Grand Rapids, Mich.: Eerdmans Publishing Co., 1971), 97, 98.

5. Ibid., 25.

6. Jer. Sanhedrin 4.5, quoted by Roger T. Beckwith and Stott W. Beckwith, *This is the Day: The Biblical Doctrine of the Christian Sunday* (London: Attic Press, 1978), 18.

7. *Church Dogmatics, III.4*, 54, 55, quoted in Kubo, 40.

8. Ellen G. White, "Ellen G. White Comments," *SDA Bible Commentary* (Hagerstown, Md.: Review and Herald Publishing Association, 1953), 7A:928.

9. Karen Burton Mains, *Making Sunday Special* (Waco, Tex: Word Books, 1987), 115.

10. Manning, 121.

11. Roy Branson, "A Call to Wonder," *Festival of the Sabbath,* 7.

12. Bacchiocchi, 127.

13. Manning, 16.

14. Ibid., 18.

15. Peterson, *Working the Angles,* 48.

16. *Parables, Etc.,* 5.

17. Manning, 165.

18. Ibid., 180.

19. Peterson, 50.

CHAPTER 6

1. Mains, 145.

2. Ahva J. C. Bond, *The Sabbath* (Plainfield, N.J.: The American Sabbath Tract Society, 1925), 39.

3. Saunders, 31.

4. Paul Tillich, *Dynamics of Faith* (New York: Harper and Brothers,

1957), 42, 43.

5. Ibid., 42.

6. Fritz Guy, "The Presence of Ultimacy," *Festival of the Sabbath,* 30.

7. Ibid., 29, 30.

8. White, *Testimonies for the Church* (Nampa, Idaho: Pacific Press®, 1948), 6:350, emphasis supplied.

9. Abraham Joshua Heschel, *The Sabbath* (New York: Farrar, Straus and Giroux, 1951), 73.

10. Ibid., 60.

11. Bacchiocchi, 86.

12. Ibid.

13. *Church.Dogmatics* III.2, 457; quoted by J. Brown, "Karl Barth's Doctrine of the Sabbath," *Scottish Journal of Theology* 19 (1966), 423.

14. Davidson, 89.

15. Clifford W. P. Hansen, "What the Keeping of the Sabbath Means to Me," *The Sabbath Recorder,* vol. 172, nos. 23, 24 (4 and 11 June 1962): 15; quoted in Saunders, 49.

16. "The Basic Meaning of the Biblical Sabbath," *The Meaning of the Book of Job and Other Biblical Studies: Essays on the Literature and Religion of the Hebrew Bible* (New York: Ktav, 1980), 49, 48.

17. Ottilie Stafford, "These Bright Ends of Time," *Festival of the Sabbath,* 16.

18. Ibid.

19. Davidson, 87, 88, emphasis supplied.

20. A. H. Lewis, *Spiritual Sabbatism* (Plainfield, N.J.: The American Sabbath Tract Society, 1910), 102.

21. This story and the quotations are from Mains, 141-144.

22. Ibid., 143.

23. Heschel, 23.

CHAPTER 7

1. Much of the material that follows was inspired by Karen Burton Mains' book, *Making Sunday Special,* chapters 12-15. She develops the theme of the Sabbath as a sign of betrothal from Abraham Joshua Heschel, whose references will be cited in this chapter.

2. Tennessee Williams, "The Glass Menagerie," in *Interpreting Literature,* fourth edition, ed. K. L. Knickerbocker and H. Willard Reninger (New York: Holt, Rinehart & Winston, Inc., 1969), 573, 574.

3. Ibid., 600.

4. Sir Walter Scott, *Ivanhoe: A Romance* (Chicago, Ill.: Fountain Press, 1949).

5. Quoted in Mains, 155.

CHAPTER 8

1. Heschel, 52.

2. Davidson, 92.

3. Ibid., 7.

4. Mains, 164, 165.

5. Ibid., 163.

6. Heschel, 60.

7. O. J. Baab, "Marriage," *The Interpreter's Dictionary of the Bible* (Nashville, Tenn.: Abingdon Press, 1962), 3:285, 286.

8. Ibid., 286.

9. *Parables, Etc.,* 5.

CHAPTER 9

1. Quoted in Mains, 162.

2. *Parables, Etc.,* 3.

3. Story quoted by Dick Underdahl-Pierce, *Parables, Etc.,* vol. 10, no. 7 (September 1990): 1.

4. Manning, 42-43.

5. Delores Leckey, *The Ordinary Way: A Family Spirituality* (New York: Crossroads, 1982), 17. She compares sexual intercourse as the ritual of the marriage covenant to the Communion bread and wine, physical elements through which we renew our promises to belong to God and revel in his promises never to forsake us. Similarly in the privacy of our bedrooms we renew, reaffirm, and deepen, in a very earthy and human way, as human as kneading bread and crushing grapes, the covenant-vows we made publicly.

6. Paul Stevens, *Marriage Spirituality: Ten Disciplines for Couples Who Love God* (Downers Grove, Ill.: InterVarsity Press, 1989), 61, 62.

7. I have changed her order of days to correspond to the Seventh-day Adventist belief in the Sabbath as the seventh-day of the week, Saturday. This diagram is taken from Marva Dawn, 53. The concept of ANTICIPATION—CELEBRATION—REFLECTION still remains the same.

8. Davidson, 18, 19.

9. Heschel, 22.

10. White, *Testimonies for the Church* (Nampa, Idaho: Pacific Press®, 1948), 6:353.

11. Bacchiocchi, 99.

12. Mains, 140.

13. Stephen Birmingham, *Duchess: The Story of Walis Warfield Windsor,* quoted in Mains, 69-71.

14. Dawn, 34.

15. Brother Lawrence, *The Practice of the Presence of God,* trans. E. M. Blaiklock (Nashville: Thomas Nelson, 1982), 85.

16. Michael Warren, "Catechesis and Spirituality," *Religious Education,* vol. 83, no. 1 (Winter 1988): 117, 119.

17. MacDonald, *Restoring Your Spiritual Passion,* 170, 171.

18. Francois Fenelon, *Spiritual Letters to Women* (Grand Rapids, Mich.: Zondervan, 1984), 16.

19. Quoted in Mains, 175.

20. Mains, 122.

21. Ibid., 179.

CHAPTER 10

1. Stevens, 55.

2. Theodore Friedman, "The Sabbath: Anticipation of Redemption," *Judaism* 16 (1967), 443.

3. Rosh Hashanah 31a, quoted by Friedman, 443.

4. Ibid., 444.

5. Ibid., 443, 444.

6. Ibid., 447.

7. Ibid., 444.

8. Ibid. For this reason, it's interesting to note, the Jews developed the Sabbath-keeping principle that only food which was prepared prior to the

coming in of the Sabbath would be partaken of (since that was the way it would be in the kingdom-to-come).

9. Ibid., 445.
10. Ibid.
11. Ibid., 446.
12. Andreason, 44, 47.
13. Heschel, 89.
14. White, *Testimonies for the Church*, 6:353
15. Maurice Blondel, quoted in Manning, 146.
16. Warren, 123, 124.
17. Manning, 172, 173.
18. Bacchiocchi, 175.
19. Manning, 109.
20. Ibid., 110, 111.
21. Scriven, 82.
22. Soren Kierkegaard, quoted in Jurgen Moltmann, *Theology of Hope* (New York: Harper and Row, 1967), 20.

CHAPTER 11

1. Bob Welch, "New Course for a New Decade," *Focus on the Family* (January 1990), 6.
2. Ibid.
3. Ross Campbell, *How to Really Love Your Child* (Wheaton, Ill.: Victor Books, 1977), 16, 17.
4. Nancy Van Pelt, *The Compleat Parent* (Nashville, Tenn.: Southern Publishing Association, 1976), 148.
5. Dawn, 191.
6. George Bernard Shaw, "The Observance of the Sabbath," *The Seventh Day Baptist Pulpit,* no. 2 (March 1903), 1: 34.
7. Saunders, 93.
8. Dawn, 193.
9. Quoted by Hans Walter Wolff, "The Day of Rest in the Old Testament," Lexington Theological Quarterly (July 1972): 72.
10. *America's Youth 1977-1988,* ed. Robert Bezilla (Princeton, N.J.: The Gallup Organization, 1988), 16, 24.

CHAPTER 12

1. The preceding illustrations are from E. Calvin Beisner, "The Poor Among Us: How Should Your Church Help?" *Discipleship Journal* 49 (January-February 1989): 17.

2. Anna Waterhouse, "From Sea to Shining Sea: The Rural Poor," *World Vision* (October-November 1990): 3.

3. *The Desire of Ages,* 207.

4. Kubo, 46.

5. "Above and Beyond," *People Weekly* (31 December 1990–7 January 1991): 152, 153.

6. "Above and Beyond," *People Weekly* (31 December 1990–7 January 1991): 154.

7. Ibid., 156.

8. Frank Clancy, "Healing the Delta," *American Health* (November 1990): 51.

9. *The Desire of Ages,* 286, 287, 368.

10. "Update," *Signs of the Times* (October 1990): 6.

11. The list is from Kathy Johnston, "Ministers of Mercy," *Discipleship Journal* 36 (November 1986): 31.

12. Dawn, 103, 104.

13. Manning, 24.

14. Jerry Bridges, "Loving by Serving," *Discipleship Journal* 27 (May 1985): 19.

CHAPTER 13

1. "Our Poisoned Planet," *Adventist Review* (19 April 1990): 15.

2. Bachiocchi, 208.

3. Quoted in Bachiocchi, 213.

4. John Stott, *Involvement: Being a Responsible Christian in a Non-Christian Society* (Old Tappan, N.J.: Fleming H. Revell Co., 1984), 160, 161.

5. From an article by Lynn White, "The Historical Roots of our Ecological Crisis," *Science* 155 (1967), 1203-7, quoted in ibid.

6. Bacchiocchi, 213, 209.

7. Francis A. Shaeffer, *Pollution and the Death of Man: The Christian View of Ecology* (Wheaton, Illinois: Tyndale House Publishers,

1972), 74, 75.

8. Betsy Carpenter, "10,000 Species to Disappear in 1991," *U.S. News & World Report* (31 December 1990–7 January 1991): 68.

9. Ibid., 69.

10. Bacchiocchi, 205.

11. The following story is from Larry Stammer, "Blighting the Land That Feeds Us," *Signs of the Times®* (September 1990): 10, 11.

12. Thorton Wilder, *Our Town*, quoted by Don Postema in *Space for God: The Study and Practice of Prayer and Spirituality* (Grand Rapids, Mich.: CRC Publications, 1983), 14.

13. Thomas Merton, *Thoughts in Solitude,* quoted in ibid., 60.

14. *Vincent Van Gogh, The Complete Letters,* quoted in ibid., 50.

15. Annie Dillard, *Pilgrim at Tinker Creek* (New York: Harper & Row, 1973), 33.

16. Quoted by Bacchiocchi, 213.

17. Dillard, 33, 34.

18. Postema, 55.

CHAPTER 14

1. MacDonald, *Restoring Your Spiritual Passion,* 162.

2. Heschel, 3.

3. Oliver Wendall Holmes, source unknown.

4. Heschel, 24.

5. Abraham Heschel, quoted in Manning, *Lion and Lamb,* 185.

6. Quoted in Manning, *Lion and Lamb*, 123.

7. *Lion and Lamb*, 24.

8. Robert E. Webber, *Worship Is a Verb* (Waco, Tex.: Word Books, 1985), 18.

CHAPTER 15

1. Peterson, *Working the Angles,* 50, 51.

2. Webber, 32, 33.

3. Stephen R. Covey, *The Seven Habits of Highly Effective People* (New York: Simon and Schuster, 1989), 30-32.

4. Ibid., 31.

5. Webber, 37.

6. Ibid., 102-104.

7. Ibid., 31.

8. Gayland Richardson, "Prayers on a Sabbath Morning." *Adventist Review* (18 January 1990): 14.

9. Dawn, 20.

10. Charles Colson, *Loving God* (Grand Rapids, Mich.: Zondervan, 1983), 32.

CONCLUSION

1. Heschel, 29.

2. Barna, 39.

3. Quoted in Mains, 123.

4. Quoted in Saunders, 8.

Bibliography

"Above and Beyond." *People Weekly* (31 December 1990–7 January 1991): 152, 153.

"Alcohol & Young People." *Signs of the Times*® (November 1990): 7.

America's Youth 1977–1988. Ed. by Robert Bezilla. Princeton, N.J.: The Gallup Organization, 1988.

Andreason, M. L. *The Sabbath*. Hagerstown, Md.: Review and Herald Publishing Association, 1969.

Associated Press. "AIDS Deaths Plunge." *Lincoln Journal Star* (8 October 1998): 1A.

Associated Press. "Teen Smoking Rate Rising." *Lincoln Journal Star* (9 October 1998): 2A.

Baab, O. J. "Marriage." *The Interpreter's Dictionary of the Bible*. Vol. 3. Nashville, Tenn.: Abingdon Press, 1962.

Bacchiocchi, Samuele. *Divine Rest for Human Restlessness*. Rome: The Pontifical Gregorian University Press, 1980.

Barna, George. *The Frog in the Kettle: What Christians Need to Know About Life in the Year 2000*. Ventura, Calif.: Regal Books, 1990.

Barth, Karl. *Church Dogmatics* III.3, 4. Edinburgh: T. & T. Clark, 1958, 1961.

Beckwith, Roger T. and Stott W. Beckwith. *This Is the Day: The Biblical Doctrine of the Christian Sunday.* London: Attic Press, 1978.

Beisner, E. Calvin. "The Poor Among Us: How Should Your Church Help?" *Discipleship Journal* 49 (January/February 1989): 17-19.

Benson, Peter L. and Michael J. Donahue. *Valuegenesis: Reports 1 and 2, A Study of the Influence of Family, Church, and School on the Faith, Values, and Commitment of Adventist Youth.* Minneapolis, Minn.: Search Institute, for the North American Division Office of Education of Seventh-day Adventists. Silver Spring, Md., 1 October 1990, 15 February 1991.

Bond, Ahva J. C. *The Sabbath.* Plainfield, N.J.: The American Sabbath Tract Society, 1925.

Branson, Roy. "A Call to Wonder." *Festival of the Sabbath.* Ed. by Roy Branson. Tacoma Park, Md.: Association of Adventist Forums, 1985.

Bridges, Jerry. "Loving by Serving." *Discipleship Journal* 27 (May 1985): 16-19.

Brown, J. "Karl Barth's Doctrine of the Sabbath." *Scottish Journal of Theology* 19 (1966): 409-425.

Buechner, Frederick. *The Magnificent Defeat.* New York: Seabury, 1979.

Calvin, John. *New Testament Commentaries.* Trans. by William B. Johnson. Ed. By David W. Torrance and Thomas F. Torrance. Grand Rapids, Mich.: Eerdmans Publishing Company, 1963.

Campbell, Ross. *How to Really Love Your Child.* Wheaton, Ill.: Victor Books, 1977.

Carpenter, Betsy. "10,000 Species to Disappear in 1991." *U.S. News & World Report* (31 December 1990–7 January 1991): 68, 69.

Chambers, Oswald. *My Utmost for His Highest.* New York: Dodd, Mead and Co., 1954.

Clancy, Frank. "Healing the Delta." *American Health* (November 1990): 43-51.

Colson, Charles. *Loving God.* Grand Rapids, Mich.: Zondervan, 1983.

_____. *Presenting Belief in an Age of Unbelief.* Wheaton, Ill.: VictorBooks, 1986.

Covey, Stephen R. *The Seven Habits of Highly Effective People.* New York: Simon and Schuster, 1989.

Cowman, Lettie. *Springs in the Valley.* Grand Rapids, Mich.: Zondervan, 1939.

Davidson, Richard M. *A Love Song for the Sabbath.* Hagerstown, Md.: Review and Herald Publishing Association, 1988.

Dawn, Marva J. *Keeping the Sabbath Wholly: Ceasing, Resting, Embracing, Feasting.* Grand Rapids, Mich.: Eerdmans Publishing Co., 1989.

Dillard, Annie. *Pilgrim at Tinker Creek.* New York: Harper & Row, 1973.

Elmer-Dewitt, Philip. "The Ecokid Corps." *Time* (24 December 1990): 51.

Dressler, Harold H. P. "The Sabbath in the Old Testament." *From Sabbath to LORD's Day: A Biblical, Historical, and Theological Investigation.* Ed. by D. A. Carson. Grand Rapids, Mich.: Zondervan Publishing House, 1982.

Fenelon, Francois. *Spiritual Letters to Women.* Grand Rapids, Mich.: Zondervan, 1984.

Finley, Mark. *The Almost Forgotten Day.* Siloam Springs, Alaska: The Concerned Group, Inc., 1988.

Frankl, Viktor E. *Man's Search for Meaning.* New York: Simon and Schuster, 1962.

Friedman, Theodore. "The Sabbath: Anticipation of Redemption." *Judaism* 16 (1967): 443-457.

Gardiner, Theodore L. "The Sabbath." *The Pulpit.* Vol. 12, No. 2 (February 1917).

Guy, Fritz. "The Presence of Ultimacy." *Festival of the Sabbath.* Ed. by Roy Branson. Tacoma Park, Md.: Association of Adventist Forums, 1985.

Hansen, Clifford W. P. "What the Keeping of the Sabbath Means to Me." *The Sabbath Recorder.* Vol. 172, Nos. 23, 24 (4 and 11 June 1962).

Hasel, Gerhard F. "The Sabbath in the Pentateuch." *The Sabbath in Scripture and History.* Ed. by Kenneth A. Strand. Hagerstown, Md.: Review and Herald Publishing Association, 1982.

Hasel, Gerhard F. and W. G. C. Murdoch. "The Sabbath in the Prophetic and Historical Literature of the Old Testament." *The Sabbath in Scripture and History.* Ed. by Kenneth A. Strand. Hagerstown, Md.: Review and Herald Publishing Association, 1982.

Heschel, Abraham Joshua. *The Sabbath.* New York: Farrar, Straus and Giroux, 1951.

"If You're Not Recycling You're Throwing It All Away." Brochure printed by the Environmental Defense Fund, 1616 P Street, N.W., Washington, D.C. 0077-6048.

Jewett, Paul K. *The Lord's Day: A Theological Guide to the Christian Day of Worship.* Grand Rapids, Mich.: Eerdmans Publishing Co., 1971.

Johnston, Kathy. "Ministers of Mercy." *Discipleship Journal* 36 (November 1986): 28-31.

Kaplan, Mordecai M. "Affiliation With the Synagogue." *The Jewish Communal Register.* New York, 1917.

Kelman, John. *The Sabbath of the Scripture.* Edinburgh: Andrew Elliot, 1869.

Kubo, Sakae. *God Meets Man: A Theology of the Sabbath and Second Advent.* Nashville, Tenn.: Southern Publishing Association, 1978.

Lawrence, Brother. *The Practice of the Presence of God.* Trans. By E. M. Blaiklock. Nashville: Thomas Nelson, 1982.

Lean, Garth. *God's Politician.* London: Darton, Longman & Todd, 1980.

Leckey, Delores. *The Ordinary Way: A Family Spirituality.* New York: Crossroads, 1982.

Lewis, A. H. *Spiritual Sabbatism.* Plainfield, N.J.: The American Sabbath Tract Society, 1910.

Lynch, James J. *The Broken Heart: The Medical Consequences of Loneliness.* New York: Basic Books, Inc., 1977.

MacDonald, Gordon. *Ordering Your Private World.* Nashville, Tenn.: Thomas Nelson Publishers, 1984.

_____. *Restoring Your Spiritual Passion.* Nashville, Tenn.: Thomas Nelson Publishers, 1986.

MacNamara, William. *Mystical Passion.* Chicago, Ill.: Claretian Press, 1977.

Mains, Karen Burton. *Making Sunday Special.* Waco, Tex.: Word Books, 1987.

Manning, Brennan. *Lion and Lamb: The Relentless Tenderness of Jesus.* Old Tappan, N.J.: Chosen Books, 1986.

Miller, Keith. *The Becomers.* Waco, Tex.: Word Books, 1973.

Millgram, A. E. *The Sabbath: The Day of Delight.* Philadelphia: The Jewish Publication Society of America, 1947.

Moltmann, Jurgen. *Theology of Hope.* New York: Harper and Row, 1967.

Norman, Geoffrey. "The Rising Tide." *Outside* (June 1989): 60.

Olgilvie, Lloyd J. *Congratulations, God Believes in You! Clues to Happiness From the Beatitudes.* Waco, Tex.: Word Books, 1980.

"Our Poisoned Planet." *Adventist Review* (19 April 1990): 15.

Parables, Etc. Vol. 10, Nos. 6, 7 (August–September, 1990).

Peterson, Eugene H. "The Unselfing of America." *Christianity Today* (5 April 1985): 30-34.

_____. *Working the Angles: The Shape of Pastoral Integrity.* Grand Rapids, Mich.: Eerdmans Publishing Co., 1987.

Postema, Don. *Space for God: The Study and Practice of Prayer and Spirituality.* Grand Rapids, Mich.: CRC Publications, 1983.

Posterski, Donald C. *Reinventing Evangelism: New Strategies for Presenting Christ in Today's World.* Downers Grove, Ill.: InterVarsity Press, 1989.

Reichley, James. *Religion in American Public Life.* Washington, D.C.: Brookings Institution, 1985.

Richardson, Gayland. "Prayers on a Sabbath Morning." *Adventist Review* (18 January 1990): 14, 15.

"Risk and Promise: A Report of the Project Affirmation Taskforces." Silver Spring, Md.: North American Division of Seventh-day Adventists, 1990.

Saunders, Herbert E. *The Sabbath: Symbol of Creation and Re-Creation.* Plainfield, New Jersey: American Sabbath Tract Society, 1970.

Schaeffer, Francis A. *Pollution and the Death of Man: The Christian View of Ecology.* Wheaton, Ill.: Tyndale House Publishers, 1972.

Scott, Sir Walter. *Ivanhoe: A Romance.* Chicago, Ill.: Fountain Press, 1949.

Scriven, Charles. "Gladness in Hope." *Festival of the Sabbath.* Ed. by Roy Branson. Tacoma Park, Md.: Association of Adventist Forums, 1985.

Shaw, George Bernard. "The Observance of the Sabbath." *The Seventh Day Baptist Pulpit.* Vol. 1, No. 2 (March 1903).

Stafford, Ottilie. "These Bright Ends of Time." *Festival of the Sabbath.* Ed. by Roy Branson. Tacoma Park, Md.: Association of Adventist Forums, 1985.

Stammer, Larry. "Blighting the Land That Feeds Us." *Signs of the Times®* (September 1990): 9-11.

Stevens, Paul. *Marriage Spirituality: Ten Disciplines for Couples Who Love God.* Downers Grove, Ill.: InterVarsity Press, 1989.

Stott, John. *Involvement: Being a Responsible Christian in a Non-Christian Society.* Old Tappan, N.J.: Fleming H. Revell Co., 1984.

Teel, Charles. "The Radical Roots of Peruvian Adventism." *Spectrum.* Vol. 21, No. 1 (December 1990): 5-18.

"The Challenge of the Future." *Signs of the Times®* (June 1990): 7.

The Holy Bible, New International Version. New York: International Bible Society, 1978.

"The Year That Was . . . 1990." *U.S. News & World Report* (31 December 1990–7 January 1991): 87, 88.

Tillich, Paul. *Dynamics of Faith.* New York: Harper and Brothers, 1957.

Tsevat, Matitiahu. "The Basic Meaning of the Biblical Sabbath." *The Meaning of the Book of Job and Other Biblical Studies: Essays on the Literature and Religion of the Hebrew Bible.* New York: Ktav, 1980.

"Two Working Parents." *Signs of the Times®* (September 1990): 7.

"Update." *Signs of the Times®* (August–November 1990).

Van Pelt, Nancy. *The Compleat Parent.* Nashville, Tenn.: Southern Publishing Association, 1976.

Warren, Michael. "Catechesis and Spirituality." *Religious Education.* Vol. 83, No. 1 (Winter 1988): 116-132.

Waterhouse, Anna. "From Sea to Shining Sea: The Rural Poor." *WORLD VISION* (October–November 1990): 3.

Webber, Robert E. *Worship Is a Verb.* Waco, Tex.: Word Books, 1985.

Webster's Collegiate Dictionary, fifth edition. Springfield, Mass.: G. & C. Merriam Co., 1936.

Welch, Bob. "New Course for a New Decade." Focus on the Family (January 1990): 6-8.

White, Ellen G. *Education.* Nampa, Idaho: Pacific Press®, 1952.

_____. "Ellen G. White Comments," *SDA Bible Commentary.* Vol. 7A. Hagerstown, Md.: Review and Herald Publishing Association, 1953.

_____. *Patriarchs and Prophets.* Nampa, Idaho: Pacific Press®, 1958.

_____. *Testimonies for the Church.* Vols. 3 and 6. Nampa, Idaho: Pacific Press®, 1948.

_____. *The Desire of Ages.* Nampa, Idaho: Pacific Press®, 1940.

_____. *The Great Controversy Between Christ and Satan.* Nampa, Idaho: Pacific Press®, 1950.

Lynn White. "The Historical Roots of our Ecological Crisis." *Science* 155 (1967) : 1203-7.

Williams, Tennessee. "The Glass Menagerie." *Interpreting Literature,* fourth edition. Ed. by K. L. Knickerbocker and H. Willard Reninger. New York: Holt, Rinehart and Winston, Inc., 1969.

Wilson, Neal C. "GC Leaders Target Concerns for the Adventist Church." *Adventist Review* (26 July–2 August 1990): 10-12.

Wolff, Hans Walter. "The Day of Rest in the Old Testament." *Lexington Theological Quarterly* (July 1972): 65-76.

Woodbury, Richard. "Eeeeyyooowiiii!!!" *Time* (6 August 1990): 3, 60-62.

Yancey, Philip. *Disappointment With God.* Grand Rapids, Mich.: Zondervan Publishing House, 1988.

Zackrison, Edwin. "A Day to Remember." *Signs of the Times®* (July 1990): 20, 21.